How I Made My Dorm My Office

Experiences of a Collegiate Student Athlete and Entrepreneur

Brendan Scott Ecker

Copyright © 2023

All rights reserved.

ISBN: 978-1-916787-56-8

All rights reserved. No part of this publication may be reproduced, distributed, or transmitted in any form or by any means, including photocopying, recording, or other electronic or mechanical methods, without the author's prior written permission, except in the case of brief quotations embodied in critical reviews and certain other non-commercial uses permitted by copyright law. For permission requests, please get in touch with the author.

Contents

Dedication i
Acknowledgments ii
About the Author v
Introduction 1
Chapter 1: Destiny - The Potential of Future Generations . 8
Chapter 2: High School to College - The Transition 25
Chapter 3: Self-Awareness - Mastering Independence 53
Chapter 4: Gratitude - Perception is Reality 65
Chapter 5: Student Athlete - Living the Label 75
Chapter 6: Making Cash Without the Sash - The Entrepreneurial Advantage 88
Chapter 7: Experiences in Real Estate - The Patience Business 109
Chapter 8: Human Nature - Insight to Human Evolution and Influential Thought.. 114
Chapter 9: A Salute to Law Enforcement- Internship Experiences and Other Stories 128
Chapter 10: Networking: Building Connections............. 141
Chapter 11: Relationships - The Golden Rule, Long Distance, Trust, & Due Diligence 146
Chapter 12: 24 House: Engineering Your Schedule 155
Chapter 13: Dodging the Freshman Fifteen: Maintaining Physical Balance 171
Chapter 14: Proving Them Wrong - Patience and Process 176
Chapter 15: Creating a Legacy - How Do You Want To Be Remembered? 181
References 185

Dedication

This book is dedicated to the Visionary, the student, the athlete, the artist, and the working man. To the entrepreneur, the misfit, the warrior, the caretaker, the teacher, and the courageous who strive to change the world and mark their names in the history books in some way.

This book is a dedication to those who venture into darkness with Valor, Wisdom, and the amor of God. To those who choose to fight, rather than to falter. Who dare to explore the unknown, and to challenge the limitations and norms set by the minds of man. To those who live by their own accord, and refuse to die a spectator or squanderer.

This book is to those who break the rules in order to break the barriers. To those who are fearless and eager to go beyond the stars - to see what has never been seen before. To those who live for Abundance, Achievement, Adventure, Advancement, Knowledge, Innovation, Justice, Transcendence, Freedom, and Truth. You are the origin of Greatness, and a representation of life's very purpose. May God grant you the riches your heart desires most.

Acknowledgments

They say to never forget the people who made you who you are. With that being said, I want to begin by thanking my Mother, Jennifer Lyn McKelvie, for always remaining by my side through the success and the struggles. Although we've had our fair share of disagreements, as any normal family does, your wisdom and love will never die. I am thankful for all of the lessons you have taught me.

As a former collegiate student athlete, entrepreneur, and police officer with much to learn still, my Mother is the reason I am who I am today. In living through adolescence of working-class hardship, I watched my Mother work as hard as any woman could so that I could do all of the amazing things that other kids got to do. Not only did she sacrifice practically her entire independent life, but she also went the extra mile and dedicated her heart and soul to my success as a student-athlete and adult during my years of academics, football, baseball, powerlifting, getting through the police academy, getting hired as a police officer, becoming a successful author, and an accomplished entrepreneur - along with so many other hard-earned Successes in my life.

The hours upon hours of hard work never mattered to my Mother. Being a financial controller for a small automotive company, she was constantly stressed at work handling the responsibility of millions of dollars, day after day, for 27 years and counting, while also having to please numerous professional and highly respected business owners. If she was told to account for 2 million dollars for her company, she would be sure to sufficiently account for every single dollar and put in even more work than requested after the job was done.

If she needed to leave work early to take me to one of my games, tryouts meet, showcases, combines, or police academy prequalification events; then she was going to get me there, Hell or high waters. She has always been my Mom and Dad growing up and is also a major reason I have succeeded to the extent I have thus far. Through every peak and valley, and through every time my character was doubted, she was there to provide constant support.

I would also like to thank my Grandmother, Betty Jean McKelvie, for teaching me the tool of never losing faith in a power higher than myself and never losing sight of my dreams. I am blessed to have been her Grandson, and I will forever carry so many of her teachings and will forever remember the values she taught me to carry.

Last but not least, I, of course, would like to thank my coaches for teaching me how to win in life and how to accomplish any goal or mission through adversity and dominating my work ethic.

For those reading, I implore you to show your parents, role model, mentor, or legal guardian the recognition and acknowledgment they all deserve, as family and the leadership that stems from them is forever, and about the memories and lessons we take from them. Without our parents and/or role models, we would not have the luxury of living in an era of fast-traveling information, improved communication, increased acceptance towards our fellow man, and the ability to interpret right from wrong on top of all the benefits of living in the 21st century.

About the Author

Brendan Scott Ecker is a renowned entrepreneur, investor, police officer, and author. He is also the host of The Brendan Ecker Influence podcast. Brendan first wrote this book, How I Made My Dorm My Office: Experiences of a Collegiate Student-Athlete and Entrepreneur, as a Junior in college in 2019. This book is one of his more interesting books, as it was later edited and released in 2023. As you will find in this book, Brendan had predicted his future of becoming a police officer and successful entrepreneur. In a way, it is one of his more captivating success stories and living proof that the manifestation of your goals is perhaps a very real phenomenon.

This book is not, however, about Brendan's career in Law Enforcement. His experiences as a sheriff's deputy and police officer can be better learned in his other book, Beyond the Beat: A Guide to Success from a Police Officer and Entrepreneur.

In this particular book you are currently reading, you will learn about Brendan's experiences as a collegiate student-athlete and what he learned about how to be successful in becoming a student-athlete while also broadening his horizons as an entrepreneur, author, investor, and overall leader.

Brendan Ecker grew up in a small town in the thumb of Michigan, where he was raised by his single mother, Jennifer Lyn McKelvie, to who Brendan has given much of his credit in becoming the public figure he is today. He was a multi-sport athlete throughout his entire life up to his time at the University of Olivet, where he received his Bachelor's Degree in Criminal Justice.

Upon Brendan's graduation from the University of Olivet, he then went on to graduate from two consecutive police academies, eventually becoming a sheriff's deputy and police officer. It was at this point in Brendan's life that he wanted to "do something bigger" to help people; where he believed that becoming an author and media personality would be a better way to help the masses "in a more indirect way".

Today, Brendan is a highly followed public figure, entrepreneur, author, and podcast host; where he also runs his YouTube channel, "The Brendan Ecker Influence", where he discusses how to succeed and accomplish your dreams while developing multiple income streams. Brendan has been outspoken about expanding his online media presence and eventually working to sell some of his screenplays as a long-term goal.

Introduction

We are not born to be failures. We are born to succeed and evolve. We are born to create and reproduce. We belong to a generation in a time where success is at its highest opportunity despite the chaos and anarchy that lurk in every corner of the world. With the ability to clone organisms, treat cancer, send life to Mars, and generate millions all from betting on the right stock or cryptocurrency, merely anything is possible in a country of capitalism and good working-class people of all socioeconomic backgrounds and experiences. Life is a jungle. It requires tough, intelligent, and strong-willed men and women with experience and first-hand knowledge to pave the way for our youth so they can fix our errors and evolve in the same way we've done for our ancestors. To me, writing this book is a manifestation of accomplishing that obligation in a small form. As famously said, if you're not a reader, you're not a leader. It's important to read the life experiences of people who have been there and done that. Getting into a private school and learning to manage my time as a student-athlete and practicing entrepreneur is something I have experience in.

This autobiography covers my experiences during my time as a student-athlete, entrepreneur, writer, and graduate from Olivet College. This book was mostly written and finished in 2019, during my time in college, but I never ended up publishing it due to the many unaccomplished predictions made in this book. What is very interesting is that many of the predictions I made years ago have come to fruition and become a reality as I have successfully taken action on my goals and dreams. I did not hope for them to come true, I prayed, but mainly, I took action. I have come back to this book in 2023 to finally publish this critical account of my experiences as a college student-athlete, entrepreneur, and writer during the four years I attended college and eventually graduated.

The rigors of college and the life of a student-athlete require mental toughness and little things to keep your brain working. The changes from student-athlete lifestyle to adult lifestyle is fierce in a world surrounded by uncertainty and variable change. Entrepreneurs, student-athletes, and the parents of any college student can learn from my successes and failures in pursuing real estate, screenwriting, a criminal justice degree, playing two collegiate sports, writing an autobiography, becoming a police officer, and investing in assets. All of those are life lessons in self-discipline, humility, success, failure, leadership, and taking action rather than hoping for action to be made at some point.

Young minds are the backbone of what tomorrow will become, and our creativity is a product of the work our ancestors put in before us. As the author of the book "Strangest Secret", Earl Nightingale, once said, "Success is the progressive realization of a worthy ideal." Meaning that with an intention to succeed, whether it be in life or earning a college degree, chasing big goals is critical while dedicating those goals to a worthy cause. Asking the right questions, executing on time, making calculated decisions, amplifying confidence, working towards a better future, providing a service, or simply being optimistic. The intention to bring good to the world values more than one who seeks to tear down what is good. To create something that wasn't there before your hands crafted it. Passion. Focus. Will. The most important elements to succeeding in anything. Those principles have always been a common similarity to every successful person regardless of what their profession is, and it is why I've been successful in my short life and always will be successful. Call it "the secret" of success. I can only hope in reading this that you can take some of my experiences and learn from them in your journey to making it as a student-athlete and critical thinker in whichever career you chase.

    I grew up in a small working-class household in Almont, Michigan. I've been successful throughout college and sports by working hard every day and never taking a second for granted. I found happiness through the lessons I learned from failure and through realizing that failure is only normal and just a part of the process. Failure is something that's hard to accept, and you've got to be tough enough to take it. Failure is only a training session and a test of your mental fortitude. It is an important catalyst for total success. A gut check. A trial to see if you're ready to take on the bigger trials ahead. I learned to be thick-skinned because I decided I'd failed enough and that I'd also learned enough to take action and attack difficult challenges.

Success has always been more enjoyable than staying down. I was set on getting out of high school, getting into college, playing football and baseball for the NCAA (like many said I wouldn't), graduating with a Bachelor's in Criminal Justice, fulfilling this book, and becoming a police officer. With hard work and commitment to the cause and the achievements themselves, all of these things happened for me. That is because I took action and never gave up when things got tough. I focused when things got difficult, and I was industrious when I wanted to be tame and relaxed.

I was different from the stereotypical college kid in a lot of ways. I never made a lot of close friends in college like I did in high school. I wasn't in a fraternity, I wasn't a typical guy you would run into at a party, I didn't care about staying on campus, I was shyer than most, and I didn't say much. Class lectures were my opportunity to shine in college and use my voice. The batting cages were my place of peace. The football turf and the weight room were where I could transfer my aggression and all my energy from the day. The competition was fierce, with 165 kids on the 2017-18 roster at my college, and a lot of scrappy, tough kids from all walks of life were there to compete against. I loved football for that. Football, in many ways, maketh a man.

In this book, you will learn the essentials of meeting an acceptable G.P.A., using the campus to your advantage, choosing your friends wisely, overcoming peer pressure, making smart investments, and of course, how I made my dorm my office. I've never questioned what I am capable of and whether the hustle was worth it. Deep down, I've always known the rewards exceeded the risks. I've dealt with the emotional struggles of a breakup and all of the common things that sometimes can lead us astray from our destiny. I've run into dead ends in the process of building two small business ventures, and I've felt the uneasy feeling of having no money and seemingly no progress with where I was heading tomorrow. However, I've been successful as much as I've failed.

I speak about my failure more excessively because without losing, you're never learning, and without learning, you're never leading. It was for these reasons that I felt driven to document in hopes that a teenager in high school looking to go to college would pick it up one day, read it, and become intrigued enough to pursue their own dreams.

Take these resources and this knowledge, and use them to your advantage. I carry high hopes that you will enjoy but, more importantly, mirror this knowledge as you continue reading this guide to success in college and everyday life.

Humans are inherently a fallen race. We lunge at opportunities to be radical and popular for attention and gratification. We seek social acceptance and purpose. Although we don't intend to be a race with evil in our hearts or minds, it's only human nature to desire the unknown and chase the most mysterious outcomes. We chase the impossible if we believe we can achieve it. We desire money, materialistic things, love, and belonging - which, throughout a lifetime, inevitably become the source of humanity's struggle to resist evil forces. God becomes a simple logic after that. May it be for poor or grand results, the victims of blind and poor judgment are ones who don't even know they are entrapped in circumstances of evil draped in camouflage. Humans are inherently tempted by evil, but humanity's intentions are good. We are tested by evil forces because God grants humanity free will, but the ultimate adversity comes from those who can resist and endure great evil temptations because that is when humanity becomes a force of unimaginable Success and Prosperity. Tomorrow's generations are critical to maintaining a prosperous nation and a prosperous mindset all around. It is the way to getting your college degree and staying on a course you can be proud of ten years later.

Chapter 1: Destiny - The Potential of Future Generations

We can be worriers, or we can be warriors in this life. We can choose to be our best and stronger than we were yesterday or crumble when life challenges us. When pushing ourselves to be better than we were yesterday, it raises the bar for the person behind us. It sets the tone. It establishes a compass for those in need of guidance and leadership ahead. Plato once said, "Human behavior flows from three main sources: desire, emotion, and knowledge." As so, our ancestors paved the way for our success today, as we do for the generations that follow us.

In a lifetime that feels over before it starts, we desire. We search for what we emotionally connect to. We seek knowledge of the crowd and of ourselves, and we seek a lifetime of ease and success. Yet many fall short of their dreams because they don't merge their thoughts with their emotions, which would become a tool to capture success while accomplishing anything we desire beyond our wildest imaginations. As said in the Gospel of Thomas, which was later edited and never included in the standard Bible, John 16:23-24 said, "Be enveloped by what you desire, because that is when your thought and your emotion become one. You think the thought of the healing of your loved ones, and you feel the love of that thought. They become one, and that is the language that this field recognizes." This is the language of success and a language that executives from the largest Fortune 500 companies have learned to master, some without even knowing it. It is a language top thinkers on the planet, from Harvard to Stanford, understand and use to their advantage. It's not the Law of Attraction. It is the Law of Influence. Every soul desires to be a master of Influence, and one who can do so in a room of many, becomes the center of attention, the genius, the weird one, the person everybody either loves or hates, and eventually, they become the center of attraction and information - which of course, gives that individual the most power in the room. That person becomes the ultimate spectacle of the room and becomes the leader.

The destiny of each man is defined by his merits and regard for what was built before him. We can be whatever we want to be. Nothing is impossible. The struggle and time put into developing, discovering, and making dreams a reality emerged at the hands of tens of thousands of generations who came before us. Even in this new fast-paced era of quantum supremacy and corporate crony capitalism, people who know history will thrive amongst those ignorant of it. Historians become thinkers of the future and Hollywood's dream when creativity fades. We live in a time where millions of people question their destiny and what's truly important in their individual lives. They wonder about the importance of hard work and where they fit in on the map, how they can get by in a system overload of politics, academia, competition, social media, stress, health concerns, car payments, a mortgage, additional financial worries, sports, love, reproduction, and relationships. They strive to know the secrets of happiness, finance, love, academia, independence, making friends, upholding a marriage, childbirth, spending time with family, or just being a better friend. To summarize, they struggle to capture and maintain health, wealth, love, and happiness. To me, the elements and the foundation to success are most important because without giving respect to that foundation, the appreciation for hard work implemented before us can't be emphasized and implemented properly. History speaks for where we stand today. History always repeats itself.

"The purpose of pursuing a college degree and chasing your dreams is to find out who you are and what you can do to pave a strong avenue of success for generations to follow during the short time you have on Earth." That's what they tell you, but that is a lie and, unfortunately, a sick joke. The truth is college is useful for just a few important reasons. A college degree shows employers and others that you are capable of remaining consistent and staying focused. It shows the ability and dedication to show up every day, for a long period of time, and achieve a desired outcome and goal. It displays your interest, and passion, for being educated and knowledgeable. It allows others to see that you are persistent and dedicated. A college degree proves that you are committed to a goal and is an accolade that cannot be taken away from you. It is a great ranking tool for corporations when organizing those on their payroll and deciding who is worthy of climbing the corporate ladder. Lastly, in my opinion, college is most beneficial because you learn how to live alone, and you learn how easily controlled you are. My views on college are different from many baby boomers and millennials, as I believe, for the most part, that a college degree is merely just a piece of paper for any true entrepreneur or independent thinker.

A college degree will certainly prove to others that you are motivated and capable of accomplishing great things, don't get me wrong. But many in today's era, especially in my generation of Generation Z, can't believe that just having a degree entitles you to a six-figure income and a life of ease. That is false, and it is lie teachers and parents tell you when you are a kid. A college degree can only get you so far if you don't use it the right way, and in this book, I will teach you how you can use it the right way for the most benefit in the macro.

In writing this book, it's objective to talk about my own experiences in college sports and the challenges that arose for me in pursuing long-term goals and graduating successfully. By incorporating angles of psychology, philosophy, history, and my own experiences, I hope to educate those who plan on successfully getting their college degree, whether it be an Associate, Bachelor, Master, or Doctorate.

Go back to when our ancestors were sitting in empty dark houses with no electricity. No hot running water. No air conditioning on 95-degree days. No warmth in the heart of life-threatening snowstorms. Take a moment to acknowledge the amount of money that surrounds you compared to countries that suffer in third world crises. You wake up, and your hunger and thirst are not quenched. Your dreams are but only dreams, all while America is surrounded by ease and economic prosperity. During World War II, women were labeled a waste of work-hand. They were expected to be loyal housewives in the kitchen and nothing more than handy housemaids. What a fortunate privilege to be born in the United States, where women have the same working opportunities as men today and currently make up half the industry of bright, critical thinkers. In America, women can vote, fight in combat, protect and serve as law enforcement professionals, become chief executive officers for billion-dollar companies, define the precedent of Olympic sports annually, and still manage to be wives and Mothers too. The potential we've created in this land we call America is precious. It is my hope that through reading this book, you will be able to maintain this standard of living, as today, society has become brainwashed and tricked into living a substandard life to the likes of a third-world country (mainly because of the powers that be). It is your responsibility to control the outcome in order to make and keep America great before it's too late.

How fortunate we are to be blessed with so much opportunity and freedom to express whichever religion we choose to follow. What a beautiful thing that a New York subway crammed with hyper kids, a single mom, and a stressed-out firefighter from the Bronx with a homeless man looking out a window can chase their dreams and make those dreams a reality if they just work hard enough at that dream. They have the potential to build and create a world that raises the bar for the youth. Even the homeless, hopeless, and bitter man can rise from having nothing and conquer the world.

From the moment of birth, we are innocent and gifted with potential. Perfect in every way, shape, and form - absolutely and totally flawless. We're filled with youthful spirit and new opportunities. New unbelievable accomplishments to achieve. New people to inspire and people we can aspire to be like-minded in. As time passes, our innocence will naturally fluctuate. We will inevitably make mistakes. Innocence and potential, however, are restored every minute of the day in humanity by even the smallest gestures, like saying thank you to another person or waving to your neighbor.

The conception and birth of a baby's beating heart are innocence and true destiny. A baby's cry is the sole fulfillment of humanity's purpose. When a baby is born, it's the binding of heaven-like perfection and the imperfection of adults with a lifetime of sin and mistakes made behind them. A new and grand achievement. When there is a new life, the human species unselfishly expands the potential of what can be accomplished in this infinite universe. The next Einstein or Stephen Hawking could be born tomorrow. The greatest gift we have been given as a human race is our connection to one another and our will to achieve greatness even greater than ourselves. Our ability to procreate and achieve the impossible despite all odds as one species. The birth of life balances the loss of life.

The sanctity of marriage embodies the responsibility and commitment between two people. A promise of lifetime dedication and companionship is rare. A pact that two people remain loyal and united as one body for better or worse. Marriage is stable, and the standard, which proves love and commitment, is achievable, even despite the many temptations that will come with marriage. Marriage is a true test, but one that should be seen as far more rewarding than unrewarding. It is a standard to reach that can help conquer our faults individually, with our best efforts. Like any marriage, you have to have the same level of dedication and commitment towards your future and, of course, towards a degree if you should choose to get one. With dead calculated focus, with all your passion, with all your intention, and with all of your might. If you have passion, you have amazing power, and many never find a way to unlock that secret superpower.

Future generations will always have the burden of fixing the mistakes of past generations. Our ancestors will always be the railroaders and builders of the generation we will inherit. This is why both should be respected for their works and merits. What can be done today would not be possible without the foundation our ancestors laid for us. Every day, the newest generation peaks its potential and proves what people never imagined possible. Eli Witney invented the cotton gin and Benjamin Franklin bifocals. The Wright Brothers invented the first airplane, Henry Ford the first assembly line. Bill Gates, the first internet virus and software. Steve Jobs and Steve Wozniak, the smartphone. Kim Kardashian and Gary Vaynerchuck, the beginning of social media monetization, and Jeff Bezos by far the most dominant multinational E-Commerce conglomerate in the world.

We learn to fix our mistakes to the best of our ability as we further our innovation and evolution as a species. As anyone knows, what happened in the past can never be undone. The only way we can grow, learn, act, interpret, lead, and perceive is by unlocking our potential as our ancestors did in order to build a perfect society where we can reproduce, build, communicate, laugh, cry, love, discover, and coexist peacefully.

The potential of tomorrow's generation of critical thinkers will forever be more amazing and unimaginable as time and technology progress. I felt it crucial to include it at the very beginning of this book because society has forgotten its purpose and potential. It is my intention to enlighten you on this if you are one of those who have forgotten or never learned about the potential of future thinkers.

By 2060, medical technology will be out of our understanding and control completely. By 2100, transportation from the United States to China will soon be faster than the blink of a human eye. Artificial intelligence will be the superior species to humans. Space flight will be as simple as using a television remote - and the money to afford it will be paid for by a universal digital-based currency backed by gold and newly discovered rare Earth elements. Yet the world forgets that evolution and the continuance of humanity have always forced humanity to adapt to change.

In college, in business, or in any endeavor, change will happen that can destroy us if we're not intentional about overcoming adversity that comes with greatness. Life is full of struggle and "no's". Full of rejections. The truly strong in this world are those who can adapt to change to become the masters of their own universe. Winners defy the narrative that failure is permanent. They know that rejection allows the doors to open for getting the "yes" with persistence. Those who succeed in finding solutions to problems, those who know that failure is only a part of the process, and those who seek answers and ask the right questions, almost always find themselves unlocking their true potentials and passions, becoming masters of not only their own lives but the universe. You have to be like that 1% of the human race, which makes the decision to be their absolute best, doing what is required while properly maneuvering through the complex cyclical nature of life - which is failure, success, complacency, and taking action to achieve the desired outcome.

Helicopters were an invention of flight that amazed people during its development. It was said to be an impossible form of aerodynamics. The argument of lift vs drag rotation was a waste of discussion to skeptics. It would have been like telling Stephen Hawking that ice was a fire. It would have been like telling Isaac Newton that there are no laws to the universe when there, in fact, is. However, just as the first airplane proved many to be wrong about its operational efficiency, so did the helicopter. The helicopter today is nothing more than an advancement in technology compared to the new technology we have. The skeptics believed it to be out of the realm of possibility and merely science fiction. Just like the first helicopter, all technology is upgradeable and will soon be adaptable and superior to human intelligence.

With that being said, humanity will always struggle to control and regulate its capabilities over A.I no matter how vast the resistance or pushback. In the classrooms of High School, college, and the workplace, it should be a priority to remember these key facts. Colleges and universities will likely not teach you these facts. In today's world, where artificial intelligence and robotics will soon be capable of matching the awesome imagination and emotional intelligence of human beings, you must be focused on being innovative and adaptable to change rather than traditional and set in the ways of the past. If you are to college, I implore you to use A.I to your advantage and be ready for the immaculate change in the way you can be efficient in college.

It is a big decision to go to college and risk your time and money or become an entrepreneur and be ahead of the curve financially. You must be careful if you want to get a degree in today's world, where only doctors, lawyers, engineers, and professors have a relevant use for such a thing. Being a Criminal Justice college graduate myself, I still wish I had spent more of my time and money learning about business, marketing, advertising, and investing rather than taking on student loan debt and learning about far-left ideas and how to be a socialist, Marxist, and communist. College, in many ways, was a waste of money, although there were a variety of beneficial lessons I learned being a student-athlete and scholar while being a writer and entrepreneur. I am glad I received my degree and eventually became a police officer because of it. It certainly helped me get the job and land other jobs outside of Criminal Justice when I needed them. It isn't a bad thing to have a degree, but in today's world, due to the cost of going to college, it is a heavy hit on your credit score and debt-to-income ratio if you don't get the scholarship or full ride.

We are entering a new era where in order to be successful in college, you have to think bigger than the stars and be as detail-oriented as you possibly can, focused mostly on making money and escaping from the grasp of the worker/employee mindset. The college will not teach you how to think like an entrepreneur or employer. It is their place to teach you the lifestyle of an employee. This is extremely difficult to do in college, as every class is constantly working to change your thinking and make you a slave to the system of working a 9-5 until the day you die with no chance of creating generational wealth. Therefore, the most important investment is raising strong independent children to be critical thinkers and action-takers for what the world's challenges will one day bring. As new generations are born, they will be the ones to fix our mistakes. As they will also make mistakes in doing so, tomorrow's generation will build upon our work and exceed the planet's potential hundreds of times beyond your and my imaginations. You have to be hungry for knowledge always, and you have to use the brain God gave you like you're working for the Manhattan Project or NASA. Thinking like this is how I made my dorm my office.

People have the supremacy of social construct, and this, even more than the most advanced artificial intelligence, is why human beings will always wish they could remain in control over evolving forces around them. However, if humanity can seek to maintain control of ourselves and remain in control of our destiny - the pursuit of generosity, laughter, love, innovation, literature, communication, art, beauty, language, diversity, emotion, reproduction, knowledge, and the new ideas that come from all miraculous things around the world, can become attainable and built for ourselves not just the robots and digital species we have created.

We, the human race, are given the purpose to fulfill those things when we are born. We are destined to never know our expiration date, but yet still find the amazement in life for the short time we are given. I wanted to get into college and make my dorm my sanctuary for success and preparation for a future that would entail amazing riches, opportunities, and wealth. In many ways, I drank the Kool-Aid and was wrong about what college is designed to do to the average student. I had to learn how to think like an entrepreneur if I wanted to be in control of my life and in control of my future in the way that I wanted to. College doesn't teach you to think for yourself. They teach you to think for your future bosses and employers. I learned this quickly in my Freshman year of college and knew that I had to resist the way the colleges teach students to think. Making my dorm, my office was a decision I made so that I wouldn't be like every other college student and waste my time in college. I was going to use every second of it, creating a foundation for true success and a future where I could one day accomplish all of my goals and be my own boss by the time I became a police officer years later.

Humans are destined to procreate and expand so that future generations may evolve and become more than their teachers or adversaries who lived before them. Although it may seem abstract, these kinds of ideas are not given enough credit in a world of cynicism, where they should be celebrated and debated more often. These kinds of acknowledgments have to be made aware in order to unlock the incentive to win in life and appreciate the rise to greatness - doing it their own way, not the way consortiums and liberal universities want you to. You should be driven and taught how to take pride in what makes you passionate and rich, not what makes someone else passionate and rich. Your mind has to be hungry for knowledge and victory 24/7, 365 days a year. Why? Because in this life, everyone wants to beat you, and everyone is competitive. Everyone has the drive and the will to accelerate their own destiny before your own, so you better get moving and take action now.

In college, you have to be obsessed with working hard, staying focused, and pursuing dreams while staying patient enough to obtain a degree worth taking pride in. The potential of our youth and the continuance of the next generation is the most selfless and key purpose to life's meaning because it brings the chance to breed more geniuses, more critical thinkers, and more optimists, realists, and pragmatists. We are born to live and continue the human race so that it may continue to expand and evolve. If you are hungry enough to go to college, you play a role in changing the world for the sake of those future generations so that they may continue to thrive as well. Every day, we generate energy frequencies that work parallel with the Earth's magnetic field, with spectacular potential, for every generation to absorb and share in.

Success in college or in any form of business requires the most imaginative and broad way of thinking, coupled with the will to fail often, succeed more, and build a great future for yourself and the next generation. Influence, knowledge, and realistic optimism can change a millennia, and college is where the test of the real world begins and where we learn what our true talents and passions are. You learn how easily you can be brainwashed and manipulated to think the wrong way, which is the way the professors and liberal teachers want you to think.

You learn how to think for yourself critically, and not like the majority around you in college, who are mostly brainwashed and tricked into believing that a degree entitles you to wealth and success. You learn that you have to chase this on your own. You have to be strong in your own convictions and rebel against the things today's universities and colleges teach you, which, again, is to be a communist, a socialist, and a far leftist activist. You have to learn to play the game and be independent, as discussed in my other book,

"Beyond The Beat: A Guide to Success from a Police Officer and Entrepreneur," where I talk about my experiences as a two-time police academy graduate, police officer, and entrepreneur.

The transition from high school to College is an even more important time to be self-aware and full of a grand appetite for knowledge and growth. Your success in college and in the real world is based on your will to succeed alone while being open-minded to thousands who face the same struggles and the same emotions but through a different lens and diverse belief system. The challenge is finishing and completing one of the most difficult challenges and transactions, which is the college degree.

Chapter 2: High School to College - The Transition

In high school, life is primarily about football games on Friday nights, making memories with your best friends, falling in love, breaking-up, saving up whatever money you can for the weekends, and eventually making it to graduation. It's not common for 18-year-olds to be thinking about building or acquiring the next billion-dollar company, creating the latest and greatest app, finding new alternatives to renewable energy, investing in real estate, or inventing the most revolutionary software platform. But in order to be a part of a solid transition from High School to College before some of the biggest and most important transitions in life later, competing with fury and overcoming obstacles becomes essential. Like any successful entrepreneur, one chasing a college degree has to be a problem solver and able to handle the pressure. Willing to read, heed, and lead.

Throughout my Middle and High School career, I was a student-athlete who thought he had it all figured out. Before college, I had completely different plans. As I discussed in my other book, I always had high aspirations. I sought to become a professional baseball player when I was 12, then grew a desire to be a Navy Seal, then a police officer when I was old enough to join the football team my sophomore year. I had always wanted to be a police officer on and off throughout my life, but it was in high school that I committed. After learning from so many coaches and bosses who taught me to always go 100% and never accept defeat, I wanted more all the time. My ultimate drug was completing a task and bettering myself. I loved the feeling of being the quiet one, the underdog to everyone in the room, only to stun them with excellence and achievement later. Being doubted is only an advantage to a strong player or any effective team.

It means your enemies are off guard and underestimating your potential. When your opponent is cocky, that's when they are overconfident - leaving them vulnerable to the resounding upset in the 4th quarter every time. In my transition from High School to College, I needed to be tough, and I needed to have my goals in mind. The transition was more than just signing so I could play football and baseball. It was more than just graduating from High School and moving into my dorm. It was all about dedication and committing to a plan. Being intentional about learning, finishing what I started, and getting the degree so I could make my mom and my town proud.

I found it to be true in football, baseball, powerlifting, cross country, tennis, or any sport I played in High School.

In football, being 5'8 and 205 lbs was small compared to offensive linemen, who generally stood at 6'0 plus and usually weighed over 230 pounds. It's normal to be on the other side of shit-talking and alpha male complex when you're not the Big Bad John on the offensive or defensive line. When you're taller and bigger, you can stand over the little guy and puff your chest out. If the little guy can't be tough, mean, and cause havoc - then he can't roll with the land sharks. He can't roll with the linemen who carry the game and would love to push around a weak player who's scared and helpless. You bend but never break - no matter who the opponent is. I knew I had to be the little guy with a Bruce Lee mentality.

I always loved Bruce Lee as a kid, and it was important for me when going from a High School mindset to a College mindset. It meant something that a man was capable of kicking so much ass and, through such adversity, recovering from a paralyzing injury and defeating his enemy by pure will, skill, and dynamics. It proved to me that anything imaginable was possible, so long as we simply believed in the vision with everything in us. I always remember his most memorable quote, which brought me strength in some of my biggest games in high school and college, as he said, "Be like water making its way through cracks. Do not be assertive, but adjust to the object, and you shall find a way around or through it. If nothing within you stays rigid, outward things will disclose themselves. Empty your mind, be formless. Shapeless, like water. If you put water into a cup, it becomes the cup. You put water into a bottle, and it becomes the bottle. You put it in a teapot; it becomes the teapot. Now, water can flow, or it can crash. Be water, my friend." In college, similar to a police officer or entrepreneur, it's key to carry this mentality all the time. Being a college student-athlete includes an experience full of emails, networking with recruiters, passing standardized tests, dealing with mental and emotional stress, learning government laws and regulations pertaining to FAFSA, and the reality that you and your Highschool sweetheart may or may not break up.

I was 5'8" at 205 lbs, but I was fast and strong from years of lifting with the best of the best at Almont when I was playing football up to getting my Diploma. A small but quick defensive tackle; I was always hearing it. "I got your ass number 3! You're with the big dogs now! Welcome to Varsity!". The older seniors on Leadership Council showed discipline and humility to cocky underclassmen trying to steal their positions or pose as arrogant hardasses. Until you were able to clash pads with the big guys and make them look silly by speed, aggression, and a sly swim move, you were no more than an insect to a wooly mammoth. I was always looked at as an easy opponent in High School and College because of my height until the snap would come or the loaders would put my weight on the bar. That was my favorite moment for anything.

When they were thinking it was going to be an easy 48 minutes, an easy six innings, or an easy weight class, it was that moment that I always loved. I loved to strike from nowhere like a Navy Seal, like a rattlesnake. When they least expected me to be dangerous, I would strike with a kill shot and subdue my enemy, who only sought to do the same to me. I loved that moment when suddenly my focus and strategy would tire the big bad wolf so badly during the game that he'd slowly run out of breath during that 48 minutes on clock. I loved making those players suffer the worst 48 minutes of football they'd ever experienced. I loved tiring them down so badly that they'd be nearly dying before the second quarter. It's a wonderful feeling to bring an overconfident athlete to his knees and humble him, but it feels all the more right to do those things with class and the intention to go back for more.

Competition and backbone have got to be fierce in the jungle of high school, college, business, and life in the process of transitioning to anything, whether it's to the next play or the next chapter of your future. It's essential if you want to make it as a dual sport collegiate athlete or entrepreneur. It's essential in order to become a successful and happy person in general when going through the High School to College transition. You have to be both fierce with the intention to hit the ground running and excited for what you can accomplish despite the world of challenges that will occur when you go from a Senior in high school to a Freshman in college.

When I was in high school, when the freshmen and sophomores moved up for the playoff run, I took the honor of being the easy target. When it was time to volunteer to get reps in, it was my time to shine. I'd go head to head with the starting seniors at practice because they were the guys who were my idols in the weight room. I wanted to be like them. To me, they were the best, and I was raised to believe that in order to be the best, you have to beat the best. The starting seniors were my models for success, brotherhood, and leadership. I wanted to be them when it was my time to be a leader. The upperclassmen loved the "fresh-meat" freshman.

Let it be made clear, there was never hazing, but this was more about just being tough. This was about being committed and dedicated to the Unfinished Story and a mission of greatness. Married to the grind. Married to the hustle. Married to the passion.

Before August of 2017, when I moved my stuff into my dorm for the first time, and before I managed to make it to graduation after years of being a pain to teachers and ex-girlfriends, football was where I learned how to leave everything out on the field, with no regrets, and learn about the transition from childhood to adulthood. Football was more than earning a ring to flash around. It was a legacy that Almont High School believed needed to be kept protected, like the Mona Lisa. We were known for being a team that always made it to the playoffs. This was more than a team that just wanted to wear the jerseys. The varsity that the freshman and sophomores got to play with wasn't in it for fun. They believed in winning the State Championship and staying focused every second of every practice. Their motto for the season was "Unfinished Story" because of the previous 2011 team that made it to the semifinals but later fell short of the ring against Flint Powers. The 2014 Almont Raiders were undefeated all the way up to the semi-finals game against Lansing Catholic. 5 years later, in 2019, the Almont Raiders were competing at Ford Field against Lansing Catholic once more, only to fall short again, with the score being 34-17. The town had made history for being the first team in the program to make it to Ford Field for the State Championship.

If you had the balls to risk wasting valuable practice time trying to "get in your reps" with the big guys, you became blood in the water with a pool full of hungry, vicious, competitive sharks. The brotherhood and camaraderie were fierce, and the competition was high. Full of 4.0 student-athletes and sublime players who filled most of the starting positions, and some players who barely clung to the academic standards (as any team would find). The 2019 team was full of dedicated athletes who loved the game for the game and also went undefeated because they knew how to ignite their potential and passion. They made history, but the story was still never finished. Even if they had gotten the rings… Almont never stays satisfied until the next W.

In football, the best part of the game is being under the lights and packing a hard hit, knocking them down in front of their girlfriends legally and in accordance with the rules. It was the ultimate goal every football player loved, aside from scoring a touchdown or kicking a field goal. I loved the feeling of exceeding my expectations and getting the game-changing sacks when they happened. I loved being on special teams kickoff and running full force at the biggest players to try and knock them on their asses. More above all, I loved giving my 100% on the field and leading by example. Teamwork taught me manhood and life lessons my father never cared to. I became intrigued in pursuing a career in Special Forces and later public safety, very much because of the lessons learned in sports and in football.

The Navy SEALs seemed like it was the best place to match what I had to offer, being a young and cocky athlete who had an act of aggression and competitive drive. The idea of being a part of the most elite and covert military force on the planet seemed like it was no less than the greatest lifestyle and a perfect one for a patriotic young tree-climbing, gun-loving, God-fearing student-athlete who loved to be his best every day. Basic Underwater Demolition (BUDs), which is the Navy SEAL's rigorous training course famous for being the most difficult on the planet, was where

I wanted to be before I ever gained a passion for the Criminal Justice field. BUDs was held on the frigid oceanic shores of Coronado, California, and Little Creek, Virginia. It was where I pretended to be throughout most of Middle School when I would even take cold showers to train for when I graduated BUDs and made it to Arctic survival school.

I know. You can laugh. I was young and cocky like I said, but I still learned to be motivated, even being a mischievous middle schooler with no bone of fear in me. During the transition from a high schooler to a college student, you have to have motivation, and you have to develop an entrepreneurial spirit with the desire to smile and shake as many hands as possible. You have to be willing to be competitive because, as it may seem unrelatable, the drive of a Navy SEAL has to live inside of you, and you must be a practitioner to be outstanding in a crowd. In the transition from a small-town football team in a one-horse town to a big-town football team in a school of thousands, be ready to compete like Hell and market yourself. Learn to demonstrate your talents. Read books on business, marketing, advertising, psychology, and philosophy. Smile and study politics. Find ways to be attractive to the eye. Whether it be a gold watch or a suit, wear it. Once you attract the eyes, you have the window to make your impression, and if you miss it, the opportunity will go to the person next to you. Become the influence when you attract the eyes. The transition depends on you being chosen in the room for the presidential scholarship over a hundred people. Where do you start? A good start is by wearing a gold watch nobody else has or a nice, pressed suit, for example. You will attract people whether they address it or not. The handshake follows, and that's when the transition of ideas and thoughts becomes possible, thus the forming of the relationship. But a good transition needs good training and practice.

I was training every day to run 4 miles in 28 minutes or less to pass the basic PT qualifications. I wanted to graduate middle school, high school, boot camp, and BUDs, then claim the beautiful golden trident, which represented a member of the Naval Special Operations Warfare Command, or in simpler terms, a Frogman or Navy

SEAL/SWCC. I remember wishing I had a beach to train on so I could get the full feel for the official 4-mile run, but Michigan only had backroads and trails, so I would run 8 miles to balance the beating and double the work. I remember when my federation baseball team traveled to Myrtle Beach, South Carolina when I nearly died trying to outcompete my teammate like an idiot.

We were in the ocean outside of the Carolina Winds condominiums, looking for girls to talk to while we enjoyed our time away from the uniforms and 104-degree tournaments. Our parents and coaches were all with us, chaperoning and overseeing everything we were doing, making sure we weren't trying to sneak alcohol. The waves were reaching a good fifteen feet or so. It was dangerous to be swimming out from shore against the waves, and there was talk about jellyfish and sharks being in the water days earlier.

While our parents were laughing and taking pictures with their outdated iPhones, a kid on my team who was raised a football player and farmer his entire life, was swimming out from shore despite the waves as they gradually became more dangerous and aggressive, hurdling toward us harder and higher by each crashing wave. I became competitive as waves crashed at my ankles. Despite the danger my teammate and I put ourselves in, we began swimming out from shore, seeing who could go further. We challenged the waves as they hammered us and filled our nostrils with salt water. For a good five minutes, he would see me at his side, still fighting the blast of the waves, and he would continue to push forward as I did in unison. I would swim, swim, and swim, and he'd still be ahead of me, swimming for the extra yard. I remember wanting to beat him so badly that I nearly drowned, and we both came to the point of being exhausted and out of breath by the time we had reached maybe 100 yards out from shore, only to barely make it back gasping and completely deprived of any breath in our bodies. When we returned to the beach, the team and parents reacted in a mild panic, and we got the expected lecture.

To this day, we never spoke about the winner, but we share an unspoken bond of challenging nature's laws. We competed, and the waves couldn't stop us. I remember I felt like I could do anything that day and push through any wave that would challenge me. I knew that if I was never a SEAL, I could certainly go to college and crush every task that followed if I would only stay focused and driven, if I only chose to push ahead, just like I did when I was swimming through the crashing waves. When you're transitioning from high school to college, you have to fight against the waves and the hurdles that will follow the process. As once said by Heraclitus, "Big results require big ambitions." Ambitions have to transcend and manifest into applied will. You have to compete against those among you who want to win just like you. Be the outgoing and obnoxious optimist. Adapt to change. The transition to college requires the responsibility of being updated on the current year's laws on FAFSA, budgeting, making sacrifices, buying a trustworthy laptop, keeping the grades up, and emailing like you're a real estate agent. Apply all of your focus and will, then anything is achievable.

As one can see, I never became a Navy Seal. I became a sheriff's deputy for the county I grew up in my entire life, a small-town police officer, along with a successful author, screenwriter, podcast host, and real estate investor. I accomplished everything I wanted to and more, and I was able to do it because I was intentional to succeed. Interestingly enough, I made several predictions about my future in this book. The previous sentences were both written while I was still in college and not yet a police officer or accomplished entrepreneur. I wanted to be better than I was yesterday, every day. I knew I was going to become these things, so I put it into this book as if it was going to happen, and it did. I graduated from college with a Bachelor's in Criminal Justice, graduated from two consecutive police academies, became a sheriff's deputy for the county I lived in, later became a police officer for a small town, and after that, started my podcast and began my real estate investing career. Yet this was only the beginning of my journey to creating generational wealth, as E-Commerce and private equity are business models I also later found great success in.

I made the sacrifices, took the punches, spent money to make money, put in the work, made no excuses, learned from mistakes, made fewer mistakes, stayed positive, became good at everything I learned how to do, and took pride in the results - because there is no better feeling than success after all those necessary steps are taken. Maximizing your options is key if you want to find your passions and develop a strong and sturdy warrior's mindset in college and in life. You have to develop an ability to become a prospecting individual, finding any opportunities and being open to them with an open mind. It starts with your attitude and your vision.

I've always loved challenging myself and being as mentally and physically fit as I could possibly be, and I knew that mistakes would happen. I never dwelled on them. Mistakes are meant to teach us and make us better. Being a leader and attacking challenges is more enjoyable than being somebody who sulks in sadness and defeat. Misery loves company, and it's infectious. Negativity and pessimism are magnetic, just as positivity and optimism are. This was my passion, and I knew if it wasn't going to be the SEALs, it was going to be something where I was making a universal impact, saving lives, educating people, and being the first to respond in the face of danger. I was going to get a Bachelor's Degree, become a police officer, and eventually become a successful, thriving entrepreneur. I made a vow to myself that I was going to do whatever it took to become a leader in everything I participated in and to change the world for the better.

I majored in Criminal Justice at Olivet College. I chose Criminal Justice because it came with the excitement of analyzing the human mind, crime-fighting, and standing for everything that was right, along with the promise of something new and exciting to see every day. I also liked the danger of the job, as I always figured maybe it was a good way to pay for some of the wrongs I've done in my own life. I had the desire to be that guy kicking down the door, risking his life to cut down the evil that walks the Earth. I've always had a warrior's spirit, and I've always believed that I was eager to defend those who don't have a voice or who can't defend themselves. Growing up, I lived my life by modeling from the biblical King who killed Goliath, David. David, in the Biblical scriptures, was a common man and a sinner doubted by many, but later became a leader and a King among his people and one who never gave up despite his shortcomings and flaws. He was a dominating leader and a taker of his desires, letting nobody disrupt his path. He stayed focused on his perceived belief in God's vision for him. He ruled for decades because of his warrior's instinct, strength, focus, good nature, and valor and because of his Faith in God's plan. His strength and spirit were that of legends, and that was the way I wanted to live my life until my final breath. I wanted people to remember me for my drive and tenacious desire for success and bringing results, despite the abstract chaos and unpredictable nature of the universe. I wanted my fellow man to see me as a person of action, boldness, strength, honesty, passion, and valor. I would rather die a virtuous man than a man of vain and a thousand regrets.

Law Enforcement and standing for America's Constitutional platform is a high honor that I have always felt a need to fulfill and defend. This was my passion for years. To be the one who fights what defies good. It was my passion to pursue the safety of the innocent and save as many lives as possible. By earning a Bachelor's Degree, I was able to place myself in a better position of success in doing those things. A college degree is something nobody can ever take away from you, and how you choose to demonstrate that accomplishment is solely up to you.

Passion is key to the transition from High School to College. It starts when you take the initiative and get your mind in a position of what I've always called 'Goal Obsession. 'Make a list of everything you want to accomplish, add up the costs to achieve those goals, turn it into a strategic plan, and check one thing off at a time as you go. Dedicate your life to that fully, and see how long it takes you to finish the list. Napoleon Hill encouraged this strategy in his laws to master the key riches of success. Ask yourself what you'll give to the world in return for those riches, and notice the change that will fill your mind. It's necessary to suggest this because we all need some kind of direction and some kind of plan for the life we want to live. Not every college student knows what they want to do or major in. Usually, if you're creative, you can make a living out of everything you do on an everyday basis. A kid became a YouTube sensation from reviewing toys. Pewdiepie and Ninja were able to become billionaires through YouTube videos and playing Fortnite on Twitch. If you don't know what you want in life, you can't properly chase and attack those long-term goals by incorporating your everyday routine. College is a great place to develop, edit, and perfect your desired goals.

There was one peer I had the pleasure of going to school with my entire life who was the definition of a self-starter and had his focus on continuous lockdown. I talk about him in my other book. He always had something else going on. When I would go bowling with my friends, he'd be cleaning tables and making the extra dollar at our hometown bowling alley. He always had the hustle switch flipped on. Inside the classroom, when everybody else was doing an assignment, he was already a staff member and student at the same time because he constantly put in that extra work. By the time I got to college and asked this same friend for advice on starting up a business, he had already founded his own consulting and IT company while also making capital. Essentially what you should take away from this story is that if you work hard and long enough on building your passion and chasing something, you will eventually find that silver lining and find yourself accomplishing goals and being successful. I imagine this same friend is very financially comfortable today, and I'll never fail to promote acknowledgment for his wisdom and dedication to being a man of action. I've always considered him a role model in the world of entrepreneurialism.

I was friends with everybody in school for the most part, but my main group was the guys I grew up playing sports with. We were always the more rambunctious crowd and tended to make a scene in the classroom more often than not. At the time, I thought I was simply going to the military and maybe law enforcement after, so I didn't really dream that I'd ever be pursuing so many different avenues like screenwriting, real estate investing, e-commerce, content creation, criminal justice studies, or writing a book at just 19 years old. As much as I credit and love all my teachers for the knowledge and time they've bestowed upon me as great professionals, my group of friends undeniably were a crazy group to deal with, at the least, and could have settled for a little less chaos in the classroom.

After more than dozens of suspensions and detentions, I finally learned that I was actually capable of getting into college. I came to the conclusion that I should start to consider my future more aggressively, the same way I put time into football, baseball, and powerlifting. By choosing to use an approach known as extrinsic motivation, I knew my study habits eventually would become more frequent, I would make fewer mistakes, I would increase my performance in the classroom, and lastly, perfect my learning to its absolute potential. It wasn't until my senior year that I finally seemed to follow this consistently.

This changed the course of my teenage life, as I made a decision to review my habits and learn as much as I could about as many things as possible. When I began to listen more and more, I enabled myself to understand things further and engage in every conversation more presently and attentively. There's a common phrase "Treat a janitor as you would a CEO." When I was in middle school, I remember a janitor who never said much. He had a few tattoos, usually looked a little worn out from the job, and was somebody that a stranger would look at at first glance and be intimidated by. Aside from this, he was also a man who went out of his way to make conversation with everybody. Our entire school knew who he was, and regardless of the way other teachers would talk down to him, a lot of my peers actually liked him more than some of the teachers. I would notice everybody become instantly more energetic, and smiles would overtake their face when they were talking to this man. Kindness is contagious like misery, and so is negativity, so choose to be like the janitor who everybody knows and loves to be around.

Changing your habits and your communication skills enables you to change your way of thinking. In college, I learned that the opinions of our peers will always be critical, as they are what fuel the necessary diversity in society. The difference in opinion gives reason to consider all angles and think in unique and wondrous ways. We can't always be wrapped up in our own way of thinking. Change is a good thing. Without closely considering the opinions of others, despite our personal beliefs, we would never be able to sufficiently think creatively and upgrade the society we live in. We would never be able to make decisions, form scholarly journals, inscribe testimonies, and, more importantly, build facts that ultimately decide our future as a people. Always question, value, and consider the opinions of every voice, as it will undeniably make you a better critical thinker, listener, and a better person.

Between High School and College, around my junior year, I took an entire summer to attend baseball showcases and football combines in order to pursue another longtime dream, which was to play college sports and prove the doubters wrong that I could do it and do it well. As much as becoming a Navy Seal and going to BUD/s (Basic Underwater Demolition) seemed like it was everything I wanted to do, I knew that route was likely going to be impossible with my sudden change of plans due to college football and baseball entering my life. I had to consider the bigger picture and what I could accomplish from the advantages I had.

    Seventeen years old and going into my senior year, I had already attended over 17 different football and baseball showcases and college visits altogether. I had one agenda, and it was to play college sports and do something that I could leave behind. It was because of this that I, again, switched back to my first plan of becoming a Law Enforcement officer and majoring in Criminal Justice at Olivet College when I made my decision. As one could tell, I was most certainly not a kid who knew what he wanted. If it weren't for my personality of going against the odds, fighting for what I believed in, and always doing what I had to do, no matter how hard the mission was, I would have never developed a constant need to succeed at the challenges that arose. Becoming a police officer was a plan more than it was a dream, but I am glad today that I had the dedication to achieve that plan and stick to it throughout my years as a student/athlete.

In school, I had to work extremely hard to maintain a grade point average that could actually get me into college. As a student-athlete in high school, I never tried in my classes for my freshman, sophomore, and partially my junior year, as I only scored a cumulative GPA of 2.1. I had to work hard to work my GPA up to 3.2 my senior year. I was a daydreamer and class-clown who liked to have all eyes on me for the most part and never cared to reach my full potential as a student until I finally woke up and realized that my athleticism wouldn't get me by forever. I knew I needed to start being a real student-athlete. I needed to be creative, and I knew there was a way I could impact the world. I just needed to figure out exactly how and how much it was going to cost. I believe that I'll never stop asking myself this question as it drives me to constantly learn new information and perfect my mind to its absolute maximum potential. From this first spark of motivation and fire came the mistakes that snowballed out of control for a long time before life's roller coaster went back up... but we'll get to that later.

When you transition from high school to college, the first emotions you feel are a mix of excitement, fear, anxiety, and being a little homesick. It's the most genuine feeling of being "kicked out of the bird's nest" that you can get, as they say. When I first got to college, I was very quiet and introverted for the most part and really didn't talk to anybody for a few years. I liked being a mystery to some extent. I remember being at football practices, waiting for scout defense to come around, and would always critique anything that I could make just a little bit better. When my reps were complete, and when it came time for the next lineman to show what he could do, I knew my work still wasn't complete. I knew my work wasn't going to be complete until I had studied my competition and did everything I could to outwork him for that spot, or at least do my best to do so.

Granted, in life, sometimes, you may not always get that spot. You may not always get that promotion, you may not always get that well-deserved reward you've been grinding for, whatever it may be - but quitting is never an option, and nor is slowing down or settling. There is nothing wrong with a little humility in life, and it's something to never forget, period. Objectives that make you painful, sleepless, emotional, and restless - will all be worth every moment in the end. Never quit, never quitting.

In college, things change from high school, no matter who you are. You'll change your mind often, and you'll learn more about yourself than you ever have before. You'll lose friends you never thought you would, and you'll grow up faster than you could ever have thought you could, especially if you give yourself a chance to. You might be somebody who never went to a party in their life but somehow ended up in a fraternity. You could be a guy who nobody knew in high school but everybody knows in college.

Things change in college no matter who you are, so really, it's all up to you on who you decide to become. If I can do it, so can anybody else. Think about what makes you happy in life. The little things. Focusing on those little things in your day that you love could lead you to one big idea that could change the course of your entire life. Nevertheless, without being self-sufficient and independent, you will never be able to fully chase your dreams and understand what you want.

Chapter 3: Self-Awareness - Mastering Independence

Social media is another major issue when it comes to grasping moral pride and self-esteem in what we do as we figure out who we are. This is mainly because we follow celebrities, musical artists, or millionaires and obsess over what they have rather than what we have. Everybody wants to be a celebrity or business magnate and make a lot of money, but yet they don't even know what they want from gaining that kind of money or attention. We see our friends "doing better than us" and become obsessive about how people see them compared to us. We second guess ourselves and compare ourselves to others because we focus on likes and how many people click a heart or a thumbs up. Loneliness is a major issue in today's society. People become lonely without even seeing the bigger picture.

Loneliness is an easy emotion to overcome because it can be controlled. Love is essential to life. But loneliness can be conquered by focusing and taking action on your goals. The key to overcoming loneliness is by learning how to fight alone. Hard work, being generous, and being locked in on your mission to succeed can cure the hardships of loneliness. Being independent makes one close to God. If you can learn how to master the art of independence and how to live alone, you can endure the feelings of loneliness and soar beyond the stars. See the planet from the outside and consider it a playing ground of 7.7 billion people. That means there are 3.4 billion people of the opposite sex searching for the same things as you. We are too young to be lonely and fearful of human connection, as human connection can never die. Be intent on seeing the world and making an impact. Learn something from someone in every interaction. There is always something to learn. Loneliness will die in the process because you will gain a love for just being alive. Love every person as if it were your last day seeing them, and the world's love for you becomes magnetic.

Before we can address the things we want in life, we first need to understand the things we need. It's important to understand what makes us who we are. When you first arrive on campus and say goodbye to your parents, you have a decision to make right then and there. You either choose to grind, put in the work, and utilize every bit of your 24 hours constructively in some way, or you choose to put things off for another time and slow progress in whatever part of your life you are trying to improve. Being in college is a challenge because the first task of using your 24 hours constructively is being able to identify what you want and what your personal needs are. It begins with addressing who you are socially. Are you somebody that prefers the company of others (an extrovert), or are you somebody who is more shy and to themselves (an Introvert)?

I personally have been a mix of both throughout my life, but more of a leaning extrovert. If we are going by the Meyers-Briggs Personality Test, I have most commonly scored as an ENTJ or an INTJ and, from time to time, even an INFJ depending on my mood. I talk a lot about this in my other book, Beyond the Beat, because it is important thing to know what characteristics and behavioral patterns you have. You must be self-aware, so knowing your personality type and what common strengths and weaknesses you have will increase your productivity and ability to thrive in today's competitive arena. Being self-aware is an advantage in a world where few people are.

Despite what the test scores have stated, I have always believed I was more inclined to be outgoing, however. I love to drive results, lead the pack, and view the world from an analytical and objective position. I find the opinions and actions of my fellow man intriguing and fascinating. I'm very decisive and quick-brained. I have always enjoyed bringing order and success to the world around me while being open-minded to the many prospects that may arise, no matter the challenge or hurdles that stand in the way. When there are flaws in a system, I see them and enjoy the process of discovering and implementing a better way to fix those flaws. I love to solve problems and bring wins to the table. I have always been a very passionate leader, and I have always enjoyed organizing people and systems to achieve the desired goal. At the same time, I also enjoy being alone with my own thoughts and focusing on my goals and objectives. I have never been much of a partier or one to attend a concert, for example.

I ask this question as to whether you are an introvert or extrovert because, reportedly, 50-75% of the United States population tends to be extroverted based on results of the MBTI.

I've observed that there are two ways to master your independence and be the things you want to be, utilizing your own identity. As stated before, you really must seek to understand what your needs are first and whether you really are an introvert or extrovert. You are who you hang with. If you one day wake up and you suddenly build this amazing desire to meet others, become involved, and build leadership skills, then maybe you're more of an extrovert. Maybe you consider joining a fraternity or sorority to become more involved and to find what your passion really is. If you're the shy breed who prefers to work in silence, obsesses over mistakes until you know it's perfect, and requires few people around you to focus on their work, perhaps you are an introvert. Maybe you go this route along with the lesser majority. Both routes, if done with the same amount of action-taking, speed, consistency, persistence, and information, can be well rewarded if equally implemented.

In high school, I was the guy who always tried to be the center of attention and most popular. In college, I was the guy who sat in the back of the classroom, read a few books here and there, did the work I needed to, and concealed myself from the world outside of football and baseball so I could dedicate every second to building something that could one day change the way the world operated and simply help others (this book). In college, I practically made my dorm my personal office, and that is precisely why I chose this phrase for the title of this book. My sanctuary of milestones and new ideas was, in fact, accomplished in the single dorm that I lived in for four back-to-back years. Things I was going to do that nobody thought I could, were right at my fingertips, thanks to a little focus and mastering the art of independence.

Some may read the title of this chapter and misunderstand the meaning of "Mastering Independence." In order to accomplish personal objectives, what this means is to master the self-control of your actions, regardless of being an introvert or extrovert. Controlling your own decisions to protect your identity and character by putting aside the temptation when friends pressure you to go outside of your moral elements. This goes along with getting outside of your comfort zone and knowing when it may be more beneficial to not be in focused isolation but rather to be around people and use them to your advantage.

For example, let's say you are pledging to be in a fraternity at a University, in a parallel situation, competing for a job as a small business accountant. Two instances where each party is both an introvert and an extrovert. In both situations, you have an expectation of cooperating, competing, participating, and complying in order to become a legitimate, welcomed party. To what extent could you still cooperate, compete, participate, and comply without having to break your own independent spirit and do things that breach your own moral guidelines? This is a question one can only answer themself. Are you going to lie to yourself and others to get ahead? Is it really worth it to smear another's reputation for your own fortune? No, it never is, and never should it be accepted in the workplace or especially in life if we are a society that wins by hard work and pure achievement based on action and merit.

People around you matter. They should be able to trust you and never question your moral goodness because your intentions are pure and not out of spite or deceit. Choose to be an assertive but also a fair candidate for that scholarship or job position. Studies conducted by the University of Southern California researchers proved that practicing the golden rule regularly and treating others the way you would like to be treated can reward generosity and maintain a healthy social balance. You can always do a job well done and help others along the way while still remaining an independent force. What we always need to value is our independence. This doesn't necessarily mean deleting friends or people from your life and isolating yourself. It's great to have fun and enjoy new experiences in life. However, you should certainly be self-aware and never lose sight of what is going to help your own future as well. I say this because it can be easy to get caught up with a group of friends or forget about the importance of competing in the workplace the correct way. Your way.

Let's say you are competing for a scholarship at a large and prestigious University, and someone writes a manuscript that earns a standing ovation from the audience on behalf of their speech. You know this person could very well get the scholarship. Will you truly put in the work and dedicate your time and effort to writing a speech that could actually be better? Or would you be the other breed who is required to cheat, plagiarize somebody else's speech, and try to succeed in such a co-dependent type of manner?

What if you were at a party, having a good time, socializing, drinking, and just enjoying yourself when your friend asks you and some others to get in his vehicle while heavily under the influence of alcohol? All of the other friends see no issue in getting in the vehicle and rush you to get in the car. What makes us give in to our mental willpower or simply say "no" during this moment? What drives or forces us to make that heat of passion decision to either tag along or stand our ground and do what we know is right?

Peer pressure is strict of choice and willpower regardless of the excuses. Peer pressure is indeed always a temptation to fight, as being human means desiring to belong or feel welcomed by our surroundings. We are always looking to fit in or lead inside our social circles. Whether it be clothing, habits in gestures and mannerisms, body language, religious or political beliefs, attitude, or how we communicate, we always adapt to our surroundings. In other words, we will inevitably become who we surround ourselves with. You should never lose sight of what you are doing and who you do it with, given that it only takes one error in judgment in this era to screw up the next 50 years of your life.

Again, this simply means being self-aware of your decisions and taking control of your actions regardless of who surrounds you or influences you. Be the influence on others, not the one who is influenced. No matter how much you think somebody isn't trying to get better than you every single day, they are. Everyone ultimately desires to be successful and prosper, so don't fear being competitive. We all have a common goal of buying a home, raising a family, and making a lot of money - the American Dream. Therefore I ask, why should you risk your independence and risk seeing your closest friends surpass you, all because of the failure to think for yourself? As my high school football defensive coordinator always said, "Don't be afraid to be a little selfish sometimes." Although I have mastered the art of independence over time, it isn't to say that I didn't share these common temptations and experiences. I could list many instances where I have failed to make the right choices in situations where I felt cornered by friends or the wrong people and regretted it later, but for now, here's just one.

Back in high school, I had a great love for my friends. I also liked to be the cool kid, though, so this drew me to make errors in judgment fairly often. I remember when I was with my friends and, at the time, really struggled to grasp my self-control. Although I have made these errors in judgment, by no means do I encourage any person to follow these same actions. I learned from the mistakes I am about to discuss, so that is why I feel telling them will build clarity in the fact that any singular person can change and control their old habitual ways by choice and willpower. Any single person can willingly choose not to initiate peer pressure as I did during this time.

During my junior year at Almont, a small group of seven friends and I sat next to each other at our school's awards ceremony. This was an event that parents and our school's alumni would attend, and it was close to summer vacation, so students tended to act up more frequently. I always respected and cared for the alumni who had gone through the rigors of High School, so this was definitely not one of my most admirable moments as I was in high efforts to build a respectable reputation so I could play college football and baseball. I still, to this day, feel regret for the actions I primarily was the origin of. However, although this was not right, I can't say that it wasn't one of the most memorable moments in high school.

Students were to claim their awards for academic excellence and enjoy a respectful ceremony. During the assembly, because I was surrounded by my friends and wanted to be the funny one, I chose to turn on the iPhone cricket tone while one of our teachers was speaking. It obviously gained a small laugh from anyone who heard it at the time. Only minutes later, one of our other friends started laughing at something completely irrelevant to the assembly. It wasn't long before all seven of us were asked to leave the ceremony and were given applause by the audience because of our inability to control our laughter. As much as I would like to believe that we were being applauded for our good humor, I'm sure that wasn't the case. This led us to the fate of a three-day suspension ultimately, but it was truly one of my more memorable moments.

When it comes to being a leader and taking the road less traveled, what people don't understand is that it's okay to take the wrong road a few times in order to find the right one.

Mistakes made in your past can never be undone or unbroken, but they can always be a part of your character and a part of your story, which to me, has always brought solace and continuous perseverance. The truth of the matter is that nothing matters. Nothing matters besides God, your family, and the memory you leave behind. Those negative moments can either make us or break us in terms of leading by example.

To build full clarity, I willfully made those decisions because I wanted to be the center of attention. It was before I really had matured as an adult. I willfully wanted all eyes to be on me, and I willfully wanted to do what I did for the pure fact that I thought it would bring humor. It wasn't because I was surrounded by friends. Yes, we will inevitably share common similarities with those we hang out with. However, it is always in our own control to make the right decisions and think before we act. It's in nobody else's control to think for ourselves in moments of peer pressure and simply aim to do the right thing. Become independent in such a way that those around you feel the need to follow your footsteps and live a similar lifestyle as you do, rather than following the road that everybody else may choose to take. No matter who we are, we can always be independent in our actions regardless of the people we surround ourselves with. The Law of Attraction and manifestation is a very real thing.

As stated before, in school, I liked to have fun and make it a relatively fun place, but I also recognized what my own limits were when I acknowledged that I was close to accomplishing what people thought I never would. Knowing that I was so close to my goal of getting to join the 10% of high schoolers that go on to play college sports, I cleaned up my act as a student and promised myself to shut out the noise and make it to graduation without blowing my opportunities. I talk about my shortcomings not to encourage the behavior but to emphasize that peer pressure is strict of choice and willpower. The only way to overcome peer pressure is to learn from our own mistakes and gain the ability to simply say no when friends or situations test our moral limitations. Mastering independence ensures the ability to think for yourself and still have fun without having to question things in moments of peer pressure.

Chapter 4: Gratitude - Perception is Reality

Perception is reality. We have all heard the phrase, and in my opinion, it is very true and accurate. Your perception of the world will create the world you live in around you. We cannot control the unpredictable fate of the universe, but we can control the way we perceive the universe and the outcome of our daily struggle in it. Be strong and ready for the impact of anything in this life, and you will have a strong perception of the world around you. You will think like a warrior in a garden rather than a gardener in a war. Be like a Spartan ready for combat rather than a serf unprepared for it. Stress must be controlled by the mind. A lion never fears a day of hunting. He hunts for the result of survival. He is strong, and the hardships of life bring him Success. But his mind must be strong. Stress brings excuses and weakness. Be like the lion who has no fear but only the will and need to survive and thrive. Perception of the world is how we will perform inside of it. If you have a vibrant vision of the future and always add on to goals, and who you are as a person, Success will supersede stress and overcome you like a waterfall.

The outlook we choose to take on rejection, struggle, commitment, fear, or physical pain, can either be viewed from a positive or negative perspective. Key elements that either make us or break us during our darkest times are how we handle those times and how we intend to get ourselves out of them. The owner of my Mom's company once told her, "Life will be up, and life will be down. You will be up one day, down the next, and up again. It is just the way life is".

Now many could argue how viable this source is. You might be wondering how these words are even credible. From my standing, it is perfect advice. Life is like a roller coaster. Just like the stock market, life is up, down, and up again, but if paid appropriate attention to, then the quality and value of life will gradually and consistently go up over time. I've always judged success through happiness, not money. Although my Mother's company owner is, in fact, a very wealthy man, he is also genuinely one of the happiest, and that defines a successful individual to me, not money. A wealthy Indian businessman who is in touch with how to move forward in the best way is a man who I will gladly take advice from.

A study made by the C.D.C (Centers for Disease Control) and (A.F.S.P) American Foundation for Suicide Prevention stated that suicide is the 10th leading cause of death in America alone, with over 1.3 million people falling victim to it. Now this was a difficult subject to incorporate into this book, as I have lost friends from this unfortunate occurrence as well as many others surely have.

With the leading cause of suicide being various forms of depression, and because the search for treatment is so elusive, it makes finding one simple source extremely hard to find. However, from the perspective of a college student who has suffered from minor waves of what felt like "depression," I still never accepted that I was "depressed," as "depression" is only a temporary emotion no different than sadness and grief. I believe that what helped me get through my moments of temporary sadness was forgetting about my own needs and focusing on the world's needs. My perception is what built my opinions of the world. I have found that when you are sad, it is likely because you aren't doing something you know you should be doing. Either you aren't attacking a goal, you aren't trying something new, or you are letting mistakes made yesterday define who you are today. You are not focusing. As Aristotle Onassis once said, "It is during our darkest moments that we must focus to see the light."

It's a logical suggestion that limiting social media, expressing gratitude greatly, and focusing on the present rather than tomorrow or yesterday, will add clarity and comfort as it did for me. I found that rather than pondering on my mistakes, misfortunes, anxiety, or negative situations, but instead focusing on how I could help others and how I wasn't alone led to a recurring state of optimism and purpose. The best way to defeat sadness or the temporary feeling of "depression," above all else, is to attack your problems and keep your expectations low while shooting high. Many successful entrepreneurs, celebrities, or professional athletes will proudly say that attacking your goals and facing your fears is the best way to capture happiness.

There have been many studies conducted in logotherapy and psychology that believe just sleeping alone can help turn a frown upside down. The most successful studies show that treatment involving cognitive behavioral therapy, which addresses patterns in problematic thinking, helps to slow and eventually stop feelings of sadness and depression. Whether including antidepressant drugs or not, it is said to be a method that is worthy of acknowledging and trying, provided your physician prescribes something like that. In my opinion, drugs are useless. Working out, attacking your goals, and fearlessly attacking your fears will eviscerate the pain of temporary sadness in almost every circumstance.

Other studies have shown that meditation can also retract any recurring negative thoughts and stop depression before it even begins. I meditate very often. There is a reason behind this action, more than just the idea that somebody is simply mentally ill. When Robin Williams took his life, a man who brought joy and laughter to the entire world, experts believed that the source was his own personal discontent and unhappiness with himself. Feeling alone was another major cause, according to family members and friends. So in order to be happy, we must learn to be happy with ourselves and not rely on others. In the end, as morbid as it may seem, we as humans do, in fact, die all by ourselves. No matter what it is that puts you in your dark place, whether it be weight, beauty, reputation, appearance, lonesomeness, your job, finances, or emotional stress, choose to better yourself one step at a time, and notice the beauty and joy in life around you. Focus on achieving the goals you've always wanted to achieve. Get shit done, and stop being sad. There is no room for weakness in a world that will only kick you when you're down. Rocky Balboa said it best.

"The world ain't all sunshine and rainbows. It's a very mean and nasty place, and I don't care how tough you are.
It will beat you to your knees and keep you there permanently if you let it. You, me, or nobody is gonna hit as hard as life. Now if you know what you're worth, then go out and get what you're worth. But ya gotta be willing to take the hits and not point fingers saying you ain't where you wanna be because of him, or her, or anybody! Cowards do that, and that ain't you! You're better than that! But it ain't about how hard you hit, it's about how hard you can get hit and keep moving forward. How much you can take and keep moving forward. That's
how winning is done!"

If it's something you can't control physically, then accept it and make it a part of you in a positive light rather than a negative. Understand that life goes on, and every day we wake up is a great day. Be willing to take the hits and punch back. You can run, hide, or fight.

I believe that anger is a better substitute for sadness. Gratitude for what we have on our backs is key to constantly being happy when we feel at our lowest. Sure, life will lead to trying times, and we will be sad or feel hopeless often. However, the choice to refuse depression is a powerful strategy that has worked for me throughout the years in dealing with anxiety and stress from college and especially high school. There were many dark times when I felt at rock bottom when really it was all in my head. Perception is reality. The way we look at every single situation will either be a cup half full or cup half empty. In a world where there is so much negativity and cynicism, staying positive and thankful for everything we have in the present is key to finding joy and value with any circumstance, leaving you in a great position for success when the next opportunity comes up. Gratitude and random kindness are the true way to a pure life.

Change is inevitable. Things are going to happen that we don't understand, but the pain comes in a million different forms. Death, divorce, betrayal, loneliness, financial debt, student loans, illness, job hate, unfairness, constant shortcomings, and maybe even a compilation of all of those together. Pain is different for every person. The concept of pain is not worth dwelling upon. We live in a new era where kindness is seen as a weakness when in fact, it's the other way around. The truest form of weakness is holding a heavy heart of hate and negativity rather than addressing your problems and changing them with intention. If you live your life trying to bring others down, you're only exposing your greatest insecurities and weaknesses, and you will only feel them later.

The successful ones refuse to let a negative moment alter their life. The ones who win refuse to lose faith in the mission, and they keep their eyes on the prize. Winners block out the pain and focus on the fight. You can't win any game in sports or expect to lead the game in states when your head is not in it. You have to stay focused even when you are in a slump and making continuous mistakes. Making the time to write this book, continuing a consistent workout schedule, maintaining a satisfactory grade point average, later graduating from two consecutive police academies, and getting hired as a cop after taking what felt like hundreds of exams, was a major change I had to accept in my life. Change and temporary tribulations will never stop so long as you are still breathing, so understand that although change may feel scary or even life-altering, it's usually all about whether we look at the situation from a positive attitude or not. Change is simply a package deal with the game of winning. When we learn to control our emotions through change, it enables us to control the change. The cup is always half full. Refuse to believe otherwise. Remember. Happiness should never be expected. It can only be pursued, as Thomas

Jefferson said in the Declaration of Independence. So pursue happiness every waking second of the day, and stay focused on changing the world. This is how you stay in the zone and never lose. Stay optimistic, and choose to win through adversity and relentless, sagacious persistence.

Chapter 5: Student Athlete - Living the Label

Being a student-athlete is more than what people see. Parents and fans see the results of that crisp November night when we beat a team in the playoffs by just one in double overtime, but not the process. Fans will see us injured, losing, getting beaten brutally, and making error after error, but not the process. Newspapers will document the highlights, the wins, and the losses, but not the process. The label placed on student-athletes means more than just the way it sounds.

The sacrifices made, the hours upon hours of doing everything over and over again just to get it right, the standards required to be met in the classroom, and the loyalty and commitment that one must acquire to call his or herself a student-athlete, are all key components to living the label and enjoying the experience.

It starts with your mindset. No matter what you do in life, perception is always reality. If you wake up and love what you do, the hours put in and the darker days will grow easier to endure and rise above. As a student-athlete, without thinking this way, one would never be able to make it through the experience without quitting. Many could argue and call this lifestyle "only for the fame and popularity," but until the two-a-days, midnight practices, hours in the weight room, injuries, and the feeling of playing your last snap takes over your emotions - one cannot understand this lifestyle.

One of my closest friends was a sublime leader and influence in my life, being a state-contending wrestler, model upperclassman, and ferocious outside linebacker in High School football. He always had a unique swagger to back up his sweat equity. Words that would sink in deep and action that would hit heavy. To this day, I still remember his famous line I always remembered, being a shorter and usually more underestimated defensive tackle, he would always tell me, "It's not the size of the dog in the fight, it's the size of the fight in the dog".

Having remembered that, it provided my mind fuel to get hungry so I could compete, earn, and continue earning that starting position as a junior in high school.

One thing that this friend also said that hit hard was, "Love winning more than you love to lose". Although this statement is very true, as an entrepreneur or wrestler, you have to be addicted to losing in a way, no matter how much you love to win. The process is all about the losing experiences and coming back up from the bottom of the reef to the top of the top of the mountain - over and over and over again. You're going to make critical mistakes. You will absolutely fail before you succeed in most cases. People will hate, doubt, forget about you, and shame you for not being the perfect entrepreneur first starting out, and that's fine. It's not the consumer's job to stay faithful to your word if you break it. It's yours. It's all about the cycle of trying, losing, losing a few more times, then finally getting it right, and finally, winning. Winning and attacking happiness, and trying to change the planet in an astronomical way, is a great start.

    I had another friend who was one of my mentors during my years in high school football. Today he is a chiropractor and very successful and fulfilled. He was a year older than me, just like my other friend I was previously talking about, but he challenged me to be my best at all times. He was an offensive lineman, about the same height as me, and the same weight class. When I was a defensive tackle, I would always have to square up with this individual every snap. He was also a powerlifter, and I learned a lot about powerlifting from him as well. He was tough as iron and hard to beat. He wasn't like most of the Offensive Lineman I went up against at practice, who would ask me to slow down and go 50%. He always expected me to go 100% so he could get a good look.

He, too, would never slow down. He went 100% all the time and expected those around him to do the same.

No matter how pissed off everyone would get at us for going 100% at practice, we didn't care. We were in it to win it, and we were setting the standards for the amount of intensity to be expected on the field - because winning was the objective. We held ourselves accountable for every single snap. It was no different than the standards of my college football team. Improvement, success, efficiency, utter domination, and adaptation were the primary objectives. Not being comfortable, slow, vulnerable, weak, and soft. This mentor in my life was one of the true proponents on the field when it came to our team's beloved phrase, "Bend, don't break". Up to this day, when I post a video of myself squatting in the weight room, for instance, hitting a new PR, I can always count on this same individual texting me, "Get more depth, pussy. You can do better". These are the kinds of teammates, friends, and mentors you need in your corner throughout the mental, physical, and spiritual wilderness of life. You need people around you who are out to make you better and hold you accountable when you can, in fact, do better.

I first started playing sports when I was just two and a half years old. My Mom insisted I play soccer and get a head start when it came to building my social skills, and I guess you could say my athletic ability too. From that point, I continued on in my athletics throughout middle school, high school, and freshman year of college. I played pretty much every sport that I could because I loved and respected the challenge of being able to do everything and become the best I could be at it. The feeling of not knowing how to do something and then working on getting better at that thing felt way better than getting bored and regretful and never trying anything worth doing at all. By the time I was a senior, I was able to give strong opinions about the rigors between football and soccer and which sport was harder because of actually playing both. I found the significance of humility from basketball in remembering and forgetting what seemed like a thousand plays. I learned the difference between team and brotherhood after being on the same federation baseball team for seven consecutive years and being on a college team for only a couple of years.

In lue of the examples, I found that I never regretted trying and seeing what I could make of myself from them. In one way or another, being a part of those different groups of athletes taught me the value of diversifying and finding new skills. Nothing that you attempt and persistently work to get better at will fail with consistent time, attention, focus, adjustment, and action implemented towards that thing. You may fail during the process and during the practice, but the end result will be continuous growth and success. Your time won't be wasted if you seek to perfect the micro details of any and all objectives.

What made me want to always stick with sports was the challenge of commitment that it served. Being a member of this lifestyle taught me to be comfortable with being uncomfortable, and it taught me the values of teamwork and brotherhood. Teamwork, trust, and winning develop naturally over time, but earning that starting position or making your way to the top 10 in the race come with going the extra mile with the intention to be the best and finish what you started. Never undervalue the intention to be exceptional over the ordinary. Whether it be in sports, something seemingly impossible to people, a career with a desk and some headaches, a low-paying blue-collar job, or a boring day in the classroom, exceptional always supersedes ordinary.

Before I got into football and powerlifting, I played almost every sport there was to play. After playing soccer, tennis, and basketball, and continuing with baseball religiously, next on my list was cross country. It was personal that I joined the team because I didn't like the way I looked, and I didn't like the way I felt about myself physically and mentally. I hated being disrespected and laughed at after gym classes just because I didn't have abs as my friends did. They were skinny and had not an ounce of muscle on them, but they bragged about having a six-pack. I took no offense and still don't to this day because my greatest critics gave me a reason to grind and put in the work so I could be better. Eventually, because of the challenge they put on me to look better than I did, I put in the work and eventually looked better than both of them physically. I had an 8-pack and muscle on my body when they didn't one summer later.

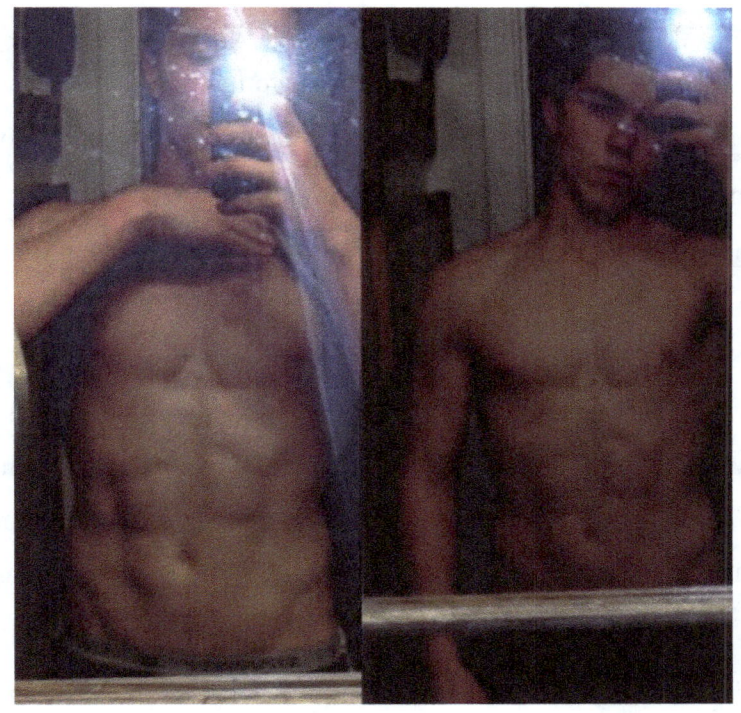

With any problem in life, rather than pondering, I focused on finding solutions and strategies to solve the dissatisfaction I had with my body as a young 7th grader. Solutions so I could fix the problems and strategies to create the system. My primary concern was how I was going to go from being a kid with severe asthma and a bad sweet tooth to a kid who ran 2-3 miles every day for an entire summer and treated his agenda as a military schedule. The answer was simple. I chose to put in the work, accept the criticism, and use it as fuel to boost my work ethic. I was committed to being my very best self as a human being and proving those wrong who laughed at me and wrote me off. After all, they were right. When I considered their opinions and perceptions of me and used them as informative fuel to reconstruct and adjust to the way I live my life, it made me stronger and more effective as a man. I did what many struggle to do when they don't like what they see in the mirror. I blocked out the pain and focused on blood, sweat, and the gain. I chose to take accountability and ownership. I decided that I was going to give them nothing to laugh at. I was going to come back looking the way they wished they could. I was going to be the standard they could never reach, all because I was going to outwork them and make them think twice about laughing at me.

Society tends to fear rejection and opposition so badly that they lose motivation or drive to even attempt new tasks or try new things. People get caught up in the rat race and compare themselves to others instead of putting their heads down and just focusing. People struggle to meditate on their strengths, weaknesses, aspirations, and fears. What is more, they struggle to intentionally change the outcome of their habitual patterns, which ultimately leads people to exactly where they are in life today. As Newton's third law states, "Every action has an equal and opposite reaction". Your daily decisions and the decisions you choose to make minute-by-minute compound and accumulate, later resulting in the place you are in life today. In other words, everything in this life is in your control, but if you are not focused and self-aware of your lifestyle patterns, then you will one day wake up and not be satisfied with the life you are living. This is your fault because your decisions and self-inflicted burdens have put you there. You must decide that it is only you who can change yourself and control the outcome. One of the hardest tasks for people to do, for example, is getting up on the first of January every year and maintaining a solid and consistent workout schedule until December of that same year. Most can't do it, and they stop after about two months. It is the most common New Year's resolution. "Get in better shape and lose weight". It is the most common resolution because your physical appearance is the easiest thing to control in your life in terms of self-improvement and controlling your daily habits. Consistency. For a struggling hip hop artist, it may be the discomfort in putting your work out there in fear that people will hate on it, despite the fact that every successful artist is looking at the new artist and saying, "Yep. I remember when I first started out. Keep up the good work".

For entrepreneurs, it tends to be the lack of sales or instant gratification that stops them from putting in the work just before the sales finally begin to come in. For the American blue-collar man or woman, it may be that struggle to wake up and break your back every day just to live paycheck to paycheck and watch 16-year-olds making $100K a month. I know this is true because it's once been a challenge for the best of professional athletes, song artists, celebrities, and even multi-billionaire CEOs and hedge fund managers. I, too, have struggled with this paradoxical, cyclical way of life that any person can easily fall trap to. Many people quit before they finally reach the finish line. Consistency. It is a pertinent element of the success recipe.

Chapter 6: Making Cash Without the Sash - The Entrepreneurial Advantage

If you want to make money in America, we live in a consumer market. There are approximately 83 trillion dollars in the global money supply when you count every currency circulating, being transacted, and printed. We live in a country run by capitalism. Presidents and politicians don't control what we do in America aside from creating our laws and organizing the policies that we Americans are constantly being asked to follow throughout every new president. Capitalism is a structure of the United States that dominates all things. When we go on Instagram, we see a celebrity or success guru pitching a new product. When we go on our laptops, advertisements pop up in an effort to persuade us to buy. On a summer day, young kids can run a lemonade stand and start their first business. Parents will host garage sales. McDonald's hires new workers and offers an hourly wage of $15.00 an hour or more. In the couch cushions we sit on, it's possible that we could find coins valued at tens of thousands to hundreds of thousands of dollars based on rarity and circulation status alone. Many don't even know that or consider it! If you were lucky enough to find a 1913 Liberty Head V nickel, your net worth would skyrocket to $4,608,650. If you were to find an 1856 S Liberty Seated Dime, you could exchange that for $15,444. We live in a consumer market where everything is for sale, where the value of things is constantly fluctuating. Therefore, we have the decision to get off the couch and become innovators rather than mindless, zombie-like consumers.

One could ask what this means to an African American who may be born into a low-income community with bad schooling and education, over somewhere like New York City, born into a family of generational wealth and various opportunities at their fingertips. It means that in a capitalist market, the young African American whose parents may either be unemployed, surrounded by friends under the influence, or trapped in a situation of debt and "unfair opportunities" for education or career choices, could if they wanted to, choose to begin studying the art of sales and expanding their knowledge of how to create their own platform of income and opportunities. Unfortunately, this is already being done in the lower income communities through the wrong ways of sales, known as drug dealing. Everyone and anyone can be an entrepreneur, but it shouldn't be through any means that could get you killed or thrown in jail, especially when there are so many other ways to become wealthy and opportunity-abundant through honest and creative forms of commerce.

Business, which used to be called "trade" back in the Stone Age, has always dominated the evolution of humanity.

As stated in the classic 1976 film "Network", "The world is a college of corporations, inexorably determined by the immutable bylaws of business. The world is a business, Mr Beale. It has been since man crawled out of the slime." Commerce has always been the catalyst for tomorrow's reality. When the U.S dollar one day dies completely, along with the YEN, the EURO, or YUAN, for example, guess what - you will still have things around you that you can trade, thus replacing the value backed by gold or a piece of paper (dollars or currency notes).

Who's to say that the young African American couldn't take a pair of sneakers or basketball cards and strive to sell them for profit on eBay or simply within their community? This attains all individuals of every socioeconomic class. Who's to say that a privileged white teenager in Queens, New York, who has little idea of what he or she wants to do in life, can't take the initiative to begin an E-commerce or social media marketing agency directly from their iPhone while sitting in the comfort of their room. Every human being that is lucky enough to have been born in the United States does, without question or doubt, have the ability to create and develop their own success through hard work and putting their mind to the test.

If you are a teenager in America who's old enough to drive a car, you've probably heard from your teachers or parents, "If you don't have a degree, you can't make a lot of money." This is far from correct, and it is a complete and total lie! The world's 500 largest companies generated $32.7 trillion in revenues and $2.15 trillion in profits in 2018 alone, and many of those CEOs were self-made billionaires. Together, those Fortune Global 500 companies employ 69.3 million people worldwide. They were represented by 34 countries. Companies like Walmart, the Sinopec Group, Royal Dutch Shell, and Chinese National Petroleum all reached almost half a billion in the year of 2019. Fortune 500 companies like Apple, Microsoft, Walmart, Exxon Mobil, and Amazon dominated the American markets, many of those executives being self-made individuals who didn't need a college degree, among many who, of course, inherited their wealth. Their passion and knowledge preceded their reputations and talents, as well as their ability to learn the fundamentals of business and the exchange of goods and services. They simply learned to understand human nature, and they understood that we live in a consumer market full of people who love to shop and spend money. They figured out what humans need emotionally and how they react to the environment and the world around them, thus allowing them to innovate products and services that have changed the course of our existence today.

Keep in mind, the revenue generated by those Fortune 500 companies could have been far greater when considering the business of private sector hedge funds, insider trading, and banker bail-outs and bail-ins, as proven during the 2008 housing market crash and 2023's depressionary period of record-breaking inflation and government overspending. Money is not impossible to make just because a college degree is out of reach. Money is the easiest thing you can make when you simply meet the Influence of another person who has money. Then can come to a long-lasting, transparent relationship where you make money together. An entrepreneur is simply a risk-taker who loves solving world issues and shaping the world around them. An entrepreneur is the greatest loser in the room because they know how to turn temporary losses into long-term wins. They are visionaries and organizers. Masterminds. They are never people who are a penny wise and a dollar short, as they say. You don't have to be the one who gets the highest scores on standardized tests to succeed. You simply need the ability to communicate and demonstrate your talents to the world while offering a service people need, whatever the service may be. You need something to sell, and then, of course, you have to know how to sell it. You need to see the bigger picture and count gains over losses. Emotionally connect to the world, and the abundance of health, wealth, love, and happiness becomes magnetic via the five elements of success in life - (1) taking action, (2) consistency, (3) persistence, (4) speed, and (5) information/knowledge.

If you meet the right person, anything is possible. If you don't have a degree, you're certainly less likely to become a doctor, engineer, teacher, judge, or highly promoted business member of any large corporation, sure. What people fail to realize is that if you're working more than you're talking, you're already winning. Money isn't hard to come by if you believe in working hard and saving money, giving yourself an edge over your friends who might be using their weekly paychecks on building a Saturday night over building a system of generating compound interest and a means of creating capital with longevity and balance. While your friends are partying, drinking, hitting the clubs, obsessing over booty calls, and wasting their time on concerts and "fun", you are investing your time and energy in assets. You are working now, so you can save enough money to start your E-Commerce store. You are saving up so you can start a YouTube Channel and influence the world. You are saving your money so you can invest in cash-flowing real estate. You are selective and do not mindlessly spend money on liabilities and wasted energy. You are not like everyone else. You are only buying business necessities and investing in your future by acquiring things like studio lighting, high-resolution cameras, green screens, editing software, workout equipment, books, a laptop, online courses to educate yourself, monthly subscriptions to streamline your business and save time, outsourcing, freelancers, LLCs, C Corps, S Corps, trademarks, business cards, employees, or of course, basic life necessities (food, water, shelter, transportation).

If you can learn, and understand enough to build your own system around the world you currently live in, then you can create an efficient means of creating cash flow, abundance, and Freedom. We don't have to work for somebody else until we are 65 years old and too old to enjoy the penalized money we've accumulated in a 401K or pension. If we chase only the money, that's when life becomes an insurmountable weight on our chest. I learned this the hard way in my very first year of thinking I was ready to take on the responsibilities of starting a company.

Being an entrepreneur weeds out those who do it only for the money and not the passion of the process. Anything you do, do it with passion, not the intention to "get rich" so you can "pay off your bills and be happy". If you're not happy with the clothes you have on your back, you'll never be able to find happiness with a million dollars. Gratitude is key, along with intelligence, patience, industrious nature, vision, focus, and relentless determination. Some of the most successful business magnates in the world, such as Andrew Carnegie, John D. Rockefeller, Lord Jacob Rothschild, Elon Musk, Jeff Bezos, and Warren Buffet, would all convey the same message to any who asked about their secrets to success in business and in life.

After trying to "start my own company", I realized that in order to start any kind of company, you need a consistent money-building system, not an X amount of money in the bank. You need a job or passive income, and you need to work every single day, both on your business and in your regular 9 to 5 job. Humble beginnings do not stand for nothing; in fact, they will make your story stand out more when you finally become rich and of substantial status and influence. You need balance and financial equilibrium so you can make money overnight. If you're a college student, this can be a challenge. Many don't have an issue finding a job in college, but many do. For me, I struggled. When college sports drew to a close in my life, I had to adapt from leaving the NCAA to finding new ways of making money as a college kid. I went from 6-hour practices, 4-hour games, and intense team weight room sessions, which would take up 25% per cent of my 24-hour day, to hours of strategic planning and research on how to win in the world of money and happiness from the lonesomeness and isolation of a single dorm. I made my dorm my office and took the time to plot my success. I didn't want girlfriends, parties, or expensive purchases. I wanted to never be financially crippled again, and I wanted to be in control of my life and destiny.

I watched my mom struggle to work long hours and still come short because of helping get me through college while my friends were spending money on new shoes, clothes, parties, iPhones, accessories, cars, clubs, concerts, and other things they just didn't need when many of them usually weren't even working to make their own money. When I did have a little bit of money to spend, I was spending it on necessities and investments until I soon got cocky and negligent of how easy it was to lose that money I had saved. I fell into the trap that 99% do before I learned what the 1% do.

I was a cocky 19-year-old freshman who felt like he was financially invincible because of the few thousand dollars he had in his portfolio. I knew how to put money in an IRA and keep my eggs in separate baskets. I invested in stocks like Tesla, Apple, Cisco, Planet Fitness, and Facebook, and I also invested in the S&P 500 index fund. I was a private shareholder in Ripple and invested in Bitcoin during my time as a freshman. I also owned gold. I had separate holdings for my emergency fund, on-demand cash, and my bank account. My problem wasn't that I couldn't save money. It was because I never respected money enough to maintain and hold onto it when I thought I had a lot of it. I began to get careless as time progressed, as foolish decisions clouded my willpower as it does for many Americans in terms of buying the wrong things and not making $100 more than you had last week, which is the practical approach.

It began with the ignorance of starting up my own small business that I trademarked and called NumeriGo. An idea for a small transport company that would offer affordable taxi services abroad. I didn't truly have all the knowledge to do it. The trademark wasn't so much of a mistake, as the trademark could always be changed by the United States Patent and Trademark Offices. I loved that I took the chance and learned from my experiences. I learned that I should have filed for an LLC, or Limited Liability Company, which was a practical way to simplify ownership of a brand name and give sole legal proprietorship while also lifting personal liability for assets and business debts. Creditors also cannot pursue any personal assets when they file for an LLC. It was one of my first lessons about being a legitimate entrepreneur. A trademark was an unwise move because it cost more than I had, and it was the beginning of the end for the couple thousand dollars I had saved up. It was a learning curve but an important one to my journey as an entrepreneur who was still just a college kid trying to build something out of his single dorm.

One of the things I really screwed up with was neglecting the long-term risk and elasticity of trying to start up what was basically a taxi company when most locations in Michigan were not willing to accept the liability involved, which would later lead to an unprofitable business and an unsuccessful one. Not to mention my lack in considering the fierce competition with Uber and Lyft. I involved friends with business when you should never do business with friends as it can often be dangerous. That "partnership" eventually dissolved. Fortunately, I had only invested $1,000.00 dollars for the Trademark, which I later dissolved due to the lack of time and knowledge I had in that market.

Months later, I got ambitious about a new idea. BossHouse. This company was meant to be motivational merchandise until I made the error of promoting it before I legally had the LLC or trademark. I found out eight months later that BossHouse was trademarked by somebody else and became registered two weeks after I first promoted it on Instagram. I learned the valuable lesson of keeping brand names to yourself until the brand is officially trademarked and used in commerce, copyrighted, or patented. The fortunate part about people, as they commonly say it, "taking your idea", is that you can always take it back if and when you make adjustments and add a little creativity and investment when your window comes to do so, provided you are financially and properly educated on the market.

Out of these setbacks, with failure to understand Donald Rumsfeld's concept of "What we don't know, what we don't know," my biggest error was when I purchased $771 worth of 100 T-shirts that I designed with a friend in college. I intended to sell them to my high school and hometown for $10.00 without understanding the rigors of building a clothing line and the difficulty in building a brand with good volume. I did not know about dropshipping and the easier ways to handle fulfillment (shipping and handling). I could have simply started a print-on-demand company and avoided the trouble of physically handling my products.

I failed to understand that buying ten T-shirts to start off with would have been far more pragmatic than buying 100 and only selling 35. I became lazy and didn't recognize that in order to sell clothes, you must be able to stay consistent, package, and ship those clothes to buyers, all while keeping books on every penny you spend on social media marketing and brand development. I didn't know about E-Commerce and dropshipping yet, as I had blindly gone into my business thinking it was going to be a killer success right out of the gate. Common sense mistake, I know.

I believe this killed a big part of my entrepreneurial credibility for a long time. When you say you're going to do it, when you say you're going to hit that deadline, and when you say you're going to create that consumer satisfaction, then you have to follow through and give that consumer satisfaction plus interest in order to gain any interest at all. Free shipping, money-back guarantees, buy one get one free, discounts, refunds… all of the above. Otherwise, you're losing respect, credibility, sales, and trust within your target audience and yourself as well. Say goodbye to scaling and growing until you fix your mistakes and bounce back a thousand times, as it often will feel like.

If an entrepreneur gets tunnel vision for the profit and not the process, failure will be the result. I made the ultimate mistake of overvaluing my own company and not being the most educated on the business itself. I wanted instant gratification, which is a common mistake every entrepreneur makes. I didn't respect the process. If you expect to grow and scale any business, you need to be the best in the business and know more about it than your competitors in the market. At the very least, you should know more about it than the people in your hometown. This will give you a fighting chance.

If you look at Uber's former CEO Travis Kalanick, resigned from CEO after investors demanded a change in leadership. He was replaced by Dara Khosrowshahi, former CEO of Expedia. The point is, if somebody can do the job better, they will be the ones to replace you. Steve Jobs, the founder of Apple, was also pushed out of his own company at one point in time by John Sculley, who was the CEO of PepsiCo before this. Later, Jobs returned as the CEO of Apple only to transfer the title to Tim Cook. So, in other words, be the best, know the most, protect the interest of the shareholders, respect the employees, secure the controlling interest, dominate the market, and compound the knowledge before making the same mistakes I did as a young entrepreneur.

Granted, this was a learning curve for me, being only 19, but I still felt as if I completely underestimated the world of business and the level of sincerity and care required. I treated a bull market as a bear market, and I spent a thousand dollars on a trademark rather than infusing the proper preparation and further research that was much needed into selling the t-shirts. I valued myself higher than where I actually was. My best advice is to always be yourself and show people that you can handle the heat of failure and get right back up and keep going- again and again and again. The beauty of being an entrepreneur is that failure and learning is the name of the game. You can make as many mistakes as you need to in order to succeed, as long as you have the money, dedication, and commitment to be humble and learn from those mistakes. If you have sagacious focus, consistency, resilience, and the ability to keep going with the end in mind, then you can't help but make a thriving, long-lasting, profitable business.

Aside from my startups, and before I became intrigued with the lifestyle of an entrepreneur, I saved up all my money from working. As soon as I stopped working, that's when money began to subtract by what seemed like a thousand dollars every month. In just one freshman year in college, I had lost about three grand worth of hard-earned dollars just by being a typical young, dumb, and hungry entrepreneur. It wasn't long before I was up at 3 am trying to scrape together twenty bucks from online surveys and scratch-off tickets. I became the American who was living off of the lottery, and eventually, I realized this was not the way to live life. Being a peasant is not ideal, and it should be an insult to any who has true self-respect. You should strive to be a King or a Queen. Like royalty, you should have the desire to shine like gold and a diamond in the rough. Be mysterious, immaculate, bold, wild at heart, majestic, wise, lovable, and God-like. Do not be the peasant, as this is a decision and a self-imposed status which can easily be controlled and prevented by careful and intentional lifestyle habits which allow for an Abundance of Health, Freedom, Prosperity, Love, and Happiness."

There is a reason some people have money and some people don't. The truth is most people overvalue what money is and don't truly understand what it is. They work their entire lives to get it, not even knowing a thing about it. They pray to win the lottery just so they can have it. Yet, they don't understand how it operates, where it comes from, where it goes, who decides the value of it, and how the money is spent. Money is an illusion. Money, in the way we understand it, is simply debt. Its value goes down every day.

Since Richard Nixon took the U.S dollar off the gold standard, it has no real value. It isn't real.

The value of money is made up out of thin air by the central banks and Federal Reserve, so they can print infinite amounts of it, distribute it to workers of the world, stamp a value of it on products and services, and continue raising the amount of debt based on its nature of inflationary construct and printing velocity. Money isn't everything. Money is no more than an exchangeable value on commodities and services and an essential tool for survival and resourcefulness. When we're 85 and in our last moments, happiness and family will be what we desire more than a couple hundred thousand or even a hundred billion dollars in an expendable variety of bank accounts.

The idea of just making that little bit of extra cash to pay off your car or house payment is so common that get-rich-quick schemes are hard to pass up when we see them advertised on Instagram or Facebook. We get more money than we know, though. Think about it. As adults, we get tax returns, inheritance, holiday bonuses, profit sharing, promotions, share in stock, occasional lotto winnings, good investments from the market, loans from the bank, credit cards, and a steady paycheck if you're like most people who are 9 to 5 employees who file a W-2 tax form every year. For college kids, half of those same benefits apply. It's easy to have and gain money. Those examples are just outside of making a weekly paycheck of $200.00-$1,500.00 a week, judging by the average American's bank account.

Money is very available no matter what excuses are made. Fear is what stops most from making more money, whether it be by taking on debt to acquire assets and liabilities or simply by getting an extra side hustle or part-time job to make more money. Our problem is that we either (A) are too afraid to take the risk and make more money by getting another job or side hustle, or (B) don't respect money enough to hold onto it in a generation where having the coolest and newest thing means everything, or partying and having a good time can't miss a weekend. Some people are doing it wrong because they rely on the lottery to change their entire life in a day when in reality, that lottery ticket would probably do nothing but test their morality and put them right back where they were before in many cases.

The American Dream is a common goal of every person, and in order to pursue and accomplish that dream, work must come first. You have to work so you can make enough money to invest in something that can triple or quadruple your income. I can't stress this enough. I was a college kid without a steady job for almost two years. I went back and forth from little jobs until the pay just wasn't worth breaking my back anymore. When I got out of football and baseball, it put me in a place of being stagnant and bored. I fell into a lot of complacency because I wasn't active and in the same routine I had been in my entire life. I wasn't used to being a college student focusing on just classes and trying to find decent employment. It was a transition that formulated the best but also the worst of times. The American Dream has become all about getting rich and replicating celebrities on social media over simply being able to provide for a family and live a fulfilled life with a healthy cash flow in the meantime. If being a celebrity is everything you've ever wanted, then that's great. Keep doing what you're doing, and keep hustling. But if you're searching for the American Dream, it shouldn't all be all about money and fame but rather about if we're happy with our current state and with our lives today, whether or not we're grateful for blessings and the little moments that matter the most.

Before college, I worked for four years with one of my closest friends at his father's farm in a small town in Elba, Michigan. Truly, there is no hard work that compares to farm work in my eyes. Much of the groundwork of the United States was built upon agriculture and manual labor. I remember waking up at 4 am to start a Saturday morning, and I couldn't believe my friend did this for a living. I would give a helping hand on the weekends, but I would always say to myself, "Yeah, no way I'm working Sunday," even though most of the time I did. We would wake up, head to their farm, about 40 minutes away from our hometown, and start stacking hay in the mound. The pay was 8 dollars per wagon, as we would typically unload about 4-10 trailers. I bought my first truck, an old Ford Ranger, from saving up my money earned on the farm, only to eventually drive bad enough to roll it after losing control on Hunter's Creek Road. My friend was with me in the passenger seat, and it was a day the two of us would never forget. We landed only two feet away from a tree and nearly died. It felt like an angel stopped the truck from wrapping around that tree, and I remember both of us talking about how our Grandfathers, on the other side, probably saved us. Whether you're religious or not, something of a higher power saved us.

After four years of farming, it was time to move forward and branch out. So me and a group of my other friends all started working at an asphalt company making $12.00 an hour, thanks to one of our buddies whose dad knew the foreman. The labor was tough, but our boss was even tougher. We walked up on our first day to approach a blue-collar man in a bandana with a lazy eye and a go-T with a bright neon-yellow traffic shirt. We were all fairly intimidated by his authoritative voice and the way he carried himself. I won't lie, when I first met him, he reminded me of one of those shady drug dealers you see in the movies and

TV shows. Regardless of this, he actually was a dedicated Christian and father who was married to his High School sweetheart.

We were all polite. We looked him in the eye, listened, and cooperated the best we could for our first summer out of high school. You could tell that our boss and his crew had worked together for 25 years. They worked faster than us, harder than us, and smarter than us, and yet they were half our age. It wasn't easy money, but we still gave our best and never complained about the task at hand, and we knew we were lucky to work at all. We would be tired, pissed off, and ready to end the day when usually we'd work two hours longer than our boss would tell us in a 12-14 hour day alone. It was cutthroat and about as dangerous as farming, but it taught us the importance of honest work and respecting the value of a dollar bill. A year later, I ended up working for that same boss after my freshman year in college, but this time I was the one taking all the screaming, shovels thrown at my forehead, and low pay for back-breaking work, which was a grueling Hell to endure.

Nevertheless, if there's anything I learned from manual labor, it's that hard work humbles us and keeps us working towards something greater in life. After two different manual labor jobs, I was drawn towards real estate because I was tired of the physical toll from asphalting and years of farm work. I wanted something clean, professional, and something I knew a lot of kids my age wouldn't try to accomplish; this was the ultimate beginning of my need to succeed and never let myself be in a position of hard labor and unhappiness when I knew I was capable of taking my destiny into my own hands and tackling happiness with full aggression and intention. At the very least, I needed to try learning the business of real estate.

Chapter 7: Experiences in Real Estate - The Patience Business

I was in my college dorm watching a documentary about Donald Trump, and I was inspired when I learned about the world of real estate and the major role it plays in the U.S economy today. That was the catalyst for my interest in not just my journey of attempting to become a real estate agent but also a real estate investor. If you're reading this now, the market is sure to have already increased. I was fascinated with the details inside of the business itself. After learning about Donald Trump's successful career in building a brand and a reputation of being a witty and audacious deal crusher in real estate, I began to build a fascination with financial knowledge and domination in executing goals along with developing the platform of success in order to win, and be what he defined as "a killer" in his book "The Art of the Deal". Trump's mindset is one of a natural "killer" in the world of business, as he says in his book, " You have to put the idea into action. If you don't have the motivation and the enthusiasm, your great idea will simply sit on top of your desk or inside your head and go nowhere." I found this to be true in every way.

When August and the beginning of my sophomore year came around, after my last summer of asphalting, a peer student brought the idea of real estate to my attention again in my business management seminar. I was a double major at the time. He was talking about how he wanted to invest in condominiums and apartment complexes. I always recognized him as that guy in the classroom that always carried a laptop around with data charts on his screen. I was hearing the words "real estate" over and over again when I would least expect it, and I wanted to know what he knew. The first thing I did when I got back to my dorm was download an app called "Real Estate for Dummies" and learn the basic language of real estate and agency law. It seemed much easier than the business actually was, though.

I searched for houses on Zillow to find something I could renovate and flip instead of going through the process of getting a license, but in order to make money, you need to have money. The problem was that I had little at the time, along with few options for work, given my college classes and football schedule. Regardless, I knew I had to taste the business and learn it to the best of my ability. Whether I was going to succeed or fail at it, the first thing I wanted to do was get educated on the basic knowledge and get my feet wet. I wanted to at least be in a position to sell homes in the state of Michigan as an associate broker, but as you'll continue to read, patience became a virtue I was forced to learn and respect above all else.

During the summer that followed my freshman year in college, I put money away to take the required 40-hour real estate course in order to get the certificate so I could later take the state exam. After two weeks of reading from Michigan's Real Estate Exam Prep book thoroughly and passing the midterm and final exams, I finally passed the class and was ready to take my state licensing exam so I could officially call myself a legitimate real estate salesperson in the state of Michigan. What followed was the process of scheduling a time and date to take the state examination, which consisted of 120 questions. You needed to answer 84 questions correctly and score at least an 80%.

Unfortunately, the first two times I took the exam, I failed miserably. The first time, I scored a 39%. The second time, after retaking and sitting through an 8-hour review course, I still only scored a 41%. It was my price for not studying like I should've and not taking the time to pay for a study guide on the Internet. Exams or any kind of test-taking simply was never my thing, and it left me with fear, doubt, and second-guessing my potential.

It was tough to come back to real estate after failing the state exam twice. I quickly learned, however, that I was still able to invest in real estate through R.E.I.Ts (Real Estate Investment Trusts), AirBnb, and standard long-term renting. I made this a priority and a main goal of mine to continue pursuing and began listening to the Bigger Pockets Podcast to educate myself on the arts of business and investing. This was after I had read "Rich Dad Poor Dad" by Robert

Kiyosaki, which gave me the insight and information needed to continue my journey with proper research and analysis. I wasn't going to give up, and I knew I was going to become a real estate investor or an agent. One of the two. It was just a matter of time. I've always been too much of a Type A personality, and it was redundant to me to just quit and go backwards. I wanted to get good at the business of real estate because I was young and hungry, and above all else, I was tired of living paycheck to paycheck, hearing about financial struggle and turmoil in my home every week, living paycheck to paycheck.

As I returned to this book in 2023 to see how far I had come since 2019, when I originally finished writing it, I felt it important to pass on this paragraph in particular. If you are in college or about to be in college, I highly recommend starting your real estate investing career early. Get a cash-flowing property and house-hack it. House hacking is the means of making additional passive income by allowing someone else to live with you on your property and pay a monthly rent. If I could go back in time, I would have done this myself. I was so busy trying to get a real estate license. I never opened my eyes to the idea of getting a cash-flowing real estate property to generate income. It would have been perfect, and I had enough to do it at this time. I would have been making money for four years rather than struggling to get a license to sell homes. Real estate is a phenomenal business, and it is one that only rewards you more the earlier you get started. So get started today and start educating yourself on real estate investing.

I call real estate the patience business because, in many ways, that is exactly what it is. Whether you are an agent trying to lock in the commission or an investor trying to close a deal, patience is key. You are going to find that properties are hard to buy and, oftentimes, even harder to generate cash flow with. Cash flow is nice, but it isn't as easy as many think. It isn't easy to lock in a trustworthy tenant or a final transaction with your buyer.

Real estate is all about patience because if you want to generate long-term wealth, then you have to take the time to save up the money, invest in renovating the home (or repairing it in many cases), find a good tenant, keeping the tenant, maintaining the property while keeping up with permits and unexpected disasters that will inevitably happen to the property, and of course, saving the money you make each month. You then have to reinvest that time and energy back into the property each month, build your equity, and then roll that money into more properties through a cash-out refinance or 1031 exchange. Repeat, repeat, repeat. Real estate is all about patience. If you can learn the patience aspect of investing in real estate or closing deals as an agent, then you can take that wealth and compound it. Additionally, then you can carry your skills of patience into the real world.

Chapter 8: Human Nature - Insight to Human Evolution and Influential Thought

Knowledge is power, and wealth is what lies in between. Throughout history, humanity has become an ever-expanding and evolving species with recurring steps towards gaining the secrets of the universe. With many questions left to surface about the mysteries such as the pyramids, extraterrestrial life, time travel, artificial intelligence, the origin of mankind, and what happens after we die, we face a constant question as to where we stand on the spectrum of intelligence in the universe. These questions we seek answers to often cause turmoil among a planet of human beings who fear the unknown, as opposed to enjoying a happy life and not fearing fear itself. The history of mankind from start to finish is similar to a 10-year analysis of the stock market. The stock market could crash, burn, cause a national depression, and induce stress and loss of value in only minutes, but later, it will inevitably grow and increase in value as when it crashes. Life is good in a sense that we will have ups and downs.

Considering today's world of intelligence, it is said in the Holy Bible that human beings were created in God's divine image and in his likeness. Does our evolution as a species come from God's divine vision of humanity we simply don't understand? Or does our evolution become tainted by the works of evil desire, testing our ability to remain righteous and faithful when temptation challenges us? It's possible that smartphones, social media, warfare, global currency, geopolitical quarrels, and mass manipulation emerge from human nature. Acts of tyranny, deception, lies, financial bondage, murder, disease, adultery, abortion, obsession for power, and hunger for knowledge all originate from neither the two entities, God or Satan, but from ourselves. Through free will and by tainting God's blessings ourselves by choice and lack of obedience and self-discipline to our subconscious mind, do we, therefore, lie responsible for our own success or demise in this universe? I, for one, believe that humanity was given a choice to create our own destiny of divine beauty or dissolve our beauty by the lust of spirit and selfish desire. We create our own Heaven and Hell based on the decisions we make every day of our lives.

From an evolutionist's standpoint, Elon Musk has made great points in the discussion of human nature and evolution. What will come next, judging by the patterns of mankind throughout history? When asked about artificial intelligence, he quoted in a symposium at M.I.T., "With artificial intelligence, we are summoning the demon," speaking on how we need to be careful and how A.I is our greatest "existential threat." He also quoted how he was "increasingly inclined to think that there should be some regulatory oversight on a national and international level" in order to control this man-made mark of the beast, as Elon claims. He often states that advancement into A.I. is a similar turning point to the evolution from Heidelbergensis and homo erectus to homo sapiens (human beings today) due to A.I's capabilities of creating its own algorithms and being able to have mindful conversations with human beings, such as the robot Sophia, created by Hanson Electronics, this issue can be one of the frightening points of conversation. Chat GPT, an AI chat bot designed for answering complex questions or drafting specific prompts, is another example of how fast AI began to take over the world.

The purpose of this chapter and the reason for bringing religion, natural selection, and innovation, such as AI, into context is to help make sense of a world that moves in what can feel like a thousand minutes per second. We live in a time that is competitive by design. It's in human DNA to succeed and accomplish more than we did yesterday. Despite the terrifying times that we as human beings may feel like we live in, times have remained the same throughout the course of history. During World War II, people believed that it was the end of the world because of the fear of nuclear attack. The Vatican and a vast percentage of the planet still believe today that Adolf Hitler was the 2nd antichrist after Napoleon, due to the prophecies written by

Nostradamus in his testimony "Les Prophéties." Below is just one of Nostradamus 'apocalyptic prophecies:

"From the depths of the West of Europe, a young child will be born of poor people, he who by his tongue will seduce a great troop; His fame will increase towards the realm of the East. Beasts ferocious with hunger will cross the rivers, and the greater part of the battlefield will be against Hister. Into a cage of iron will the great one be drawn when the child of Germany observes nothing."

Nostradamus was a Christian prophet that also predicted the 9/11 World Trade Center attacks and the death of King Henry II. Nevertheless, even after reading such accurate and morbid predictions from this scholarly prophet, here I am writing this as you today are reading it, breathing and still alive. Where there is good, there is evil. Where there is madness, there will be miracles. The Holy Bible, The Quran, or any pro-human religious text states that good always prevails over evil in the end and that "all is well." Regardless of any tragedy, according to history, goodness and hope will surely prevail and subdue evil, as did the allies against the axis powers in World War II.

A wise man in the 21st century and beyond will note that any great war, whether by weaponry and warfare, political deception, economic inflation, deflation, or creation beyond control, will later rule in favor of the class with the harder-working minds. One of America's founding fathers, Thomas Jefferson, once warned a future America about federal banks, for example, that would control currency and the people of the nation by design and without their knowledge. He stated in a letter to the Secretary of the Treasury, Albert Gallatin:

"I believe that banking institutions are more dangerous to our liberties than standing armies. If the American people ever allow private banks to control the issue of their currency, first by inflation, then by deflation, the banks and corporations that will grow up around [The Banks] will deprive the people of all property until their children wake-up homeless on the continent their fathers conquered. The issuing power should be taken from the banks and restored to the people, to whom it properly belongs."

This letter that Thomas Jefferson wrote to Albert Gallatin was a bold statement within a greatly accurate prediction made before technology and social media came to fruition. As we look at the U.S federal banks today, banks and the Federal Reserve currently inflate and deflate the stock market based on leaders in the Security and Exchange Commission (SEC).

There are many billionaires who speak about strategies for gaining maximum profit in dividends by betting on global crises, which in itself sounds innocent and harmless, but in more ways than one, is a meticulous and questionable strategy for generating wealth. Betting on crises is a great way to make long-term growth in profit, which, yes, is capitalism. On the contrary, when a country, for example, suffers from, say, a natural disaster - another country usually funds new investments in small business 'and hospital reform for the public good.

This later means more new businesses and money for the shareholder who invested in a system that was set-up for failure and unnecessary reform later. It's important to be aware of where the money goes as a taxpayer and how it's changed since America's inception. Beware of your investments and follow the dollar bill's journey. This isn't to say that all billionaires and politicians have jaded strategies of generating wealth, special interest, and agendas by any means, but it's happened before, and it happens today in far more unbelievable ways than many could imagine. Always beware of your investments. If you want the truth, follow the money.

When considering humanity's natural metacognition, human beings are wired to pursue and obtain influence and control. Influence and control over the appearance, a crowd, a lover's heart, or themselves. In some way or another, each person craves influence and control over at least one area in their life. A bodybuilder works to control their muscular physique and uses it as an influence, the same way a politician seeks to influence and control larger psychographics of people. Even within a historical timeline, influence and control have remained a primitive quest.

Sanctioned in 1953, America engaged in what many believed to be a conspiracy theory for so long, but today has been proven to be true by official declassified documents which were released by the C.I.A. MKUltra, which was a human study conducted to observe and collect information on the minds of humans in efforts to gain leverage on the war of information and influence via clandestine operations, was an example of how valued influence and control is and was. Operation Paperclip was another example of how much the U.S government has always valued information, control, and influence. America brought thousands of German scientists and Nazis to the states so we could use their intelligence to gain a technological advantage over enemies, foreign and domestic. Between MKUltra and Operation Paperclip, both of these operations are evident of the need for control and influence. The projects were organized by the Office of Scientific Intelligence within the Central Intelligence Agency. A C.I.A memo from June in the 1950's quotes:

"Hypnotism appears to have been used in some cases by the soviets. It has the possibility of lowering resistance against telling the truth while also being able to induce specific actions or behavior of the subject. It is possible for a skilled Russian operator to bring about interrogation and

leave the subject with no specific recollection of having been interrogated."

The C.I.A. has now released over 20,000 declassified documents pertaining to MKUltra, for instance. The intent of the project was to study "the use of biological and chemical materials in altering human behavior," according to the official testimony of CIA director Stansfield.

Turner in 1977. With that being said, we are living in significant times as we now have unlimited information inside of a small device that can fit into our pockets. Through Instagram, Facebook, Snapchat, LinkedIn, TikTok, and Twitter, we now find ourselves at the peak of control in what we watch, learn, and engage with when using these apps. We control what we want to use and see on the device, but we don't see how the device controls us without our knowledge of it even doing so until today. Future generations will struggle to drive from New York to California without a GPS, all because of the obsolescence of road maps. During a power outage, it will become a growing crisis for people due to the absence of technology and 5G internet to relieve the boredom of silence and intellectual thought outside of a cell phone's advanced capabilities. Constant status updates and fast information will supersede priority over our own surroundings within the next 25 years. It's vital that we be cognitive of the modifications that we silently agree to as they become natural to our everyday life, especially when artificial intelligence takes full possession over the human mind, as it is destined to do.

Knowledge, power, attention, and control are four things mankind values greater than the precious gifts such as mystery, freedom, privacy, and dignity when reading into chapter 1 of any history textbook. Since the first recorded humans to walk the earth, meritocracy has slowly grown to be the ruling form of leadership over the world. The amount of work you do is what your value is worth on a numbers basis. This has culminated in capitalism and the free market in America today, which has been proven to be the strongest form of the economy since prehistoric times when humans would trade goods and services along with land and property to provide for their families. A system that has existed and been virtually effective forever.

If America were to transition to an economic system of socialism rather than free market Capitalism, we would be allowing the dead beat fathers and alcoholics who refuse to work in this country, for example, the same yearly salary as engineers, doctors, lawyers, and entrepreneurs. We would be offering the same proportion of value to those who do not earn it. The people who build our industries, businesses, and the free market are those who should be, first and foremost, compensated for their work. In a country governed by socialism, we lose our ability to compete and eventually pay for the welfare of tax-paying Americans. This was identified when the Biden Administration chose to end Title 42, which allowed illegal immigration to soar without the ability to identify those who were coming in and out of America from Mexico. Illegal immigrants were better provided for than legal Americans were, and this was a prime example of Socialism. This was proven when the same Administration gave billions of taxpayer dollars to Ukraine so they could drag America into an unnecessary war with Russia and China.

Many believe that raising taxes on the richest of Americans would be a viable solution, but this solves nothing either, as the wealthiest earners will simply move somewhere else where they are incentivized to build businesses and donate to government projects. Raising taxes on the rich is foolish and solves nothing. If a person owns the rights to their business and makes a million dollars in capital per day, they deserve to reap the benefits of that work put in after their fair amount of taxes is already being paid. In 2023, the tax code required any person earning more than $400k per year to pay 39% in taxes. Talk about the greatest heist masqueraded as "progressive taxation" and "quantitative easing."

Logically, a 40-year-old who has no job or employment, and does not pay taxes because of that, should not be able to make the same amount of income as hard-working

Americans, like a neurosurgeon, for instance. They should not be the ones to reap those same benefits as a Neurosurgeon who does their job well and already pays their fair amount of taxes. People fail to consider the risk factors and job demand of 6 figure-paying career choices in many cases. Supply and demand are what make this fair. Consider the risk behind a Neurosurgeon's line of work. One who operates on the brain and nervous system. They are paid a handsome yearly income because their job entitles a dangerous risk of liability. One wrong action that a neurosurgeon makes during an operation could kill the human being and take their life, causing distress among the family, which would eventually lead to lawsuits likely unplayable. We must also consider the number of college pre-meds who can actually manage to become working Neurosurgeons in America versus the amount of Americans who could become Walmart greeters. With respect to the Walmart greeter, a Walmart greeter's job title does not require 8 years of schooling which brings college loan debt into the hundreds of thousands. The liability of life-risk factor for a Walmart clerk is obviously not greater than a Neurosurgeon's. Many more job positions can be filled for a Walmart greeter over a Neurosurgeon. Hence, Neurosurgeon formulaically deserves the amount of income they receive. It would not be fair to pay a Walmart clerk and a Neurosurgeon the same yearly gross income and charge the

Neurosurgeon more on taxes. This is socialism. Socialism in itself today, for my generation, seems to be either misinterpreted or arguably an excuse for Americans not to work but still be paid. It's only been a false promise to the Democratic Party when looking at the common sense of that governing system. This has been proven when looking at Scandinavia or the Soviet Union when looking back in history textbooks. The entire concept of being paid in direct proportion to the amount of work you do would be delipidated and void in a government-run by socialism. We have seen this transpire in the past 4 years.

    The argument is valid to make in this extraordinary time, as we see election periods where our Constitution is being put to its test of faith. George Soros, the man who broke the bank of England in 1992 by short-selling billions in pounds sterling for his own personal gain. He's continuously announced his plans to do it again in America "when the stock market gains momentum," in his own words, thus causing a recession by short selling on Fortune 500 companies and indexes. George Soros is one of the financiers of CNN and many other networks watched by millions every day. He also is the author of "The Death of Capitalism," "It's Not Easy Being God," and "The Alchemy of Finance." George Soros and the Bilderberg Group have been the primary financiers of making that happen on a mass social scale and have been doing it to hundreds of countries, admittedly with no remorse but rather pride, Believing they are doing the planet good by inflating and deflating the markets along with the social construct America has always thrived by.

Moving forward, we must acknowledge the times we are living in and be urgent of the choices we make in terms of how things can affect us as a mass society. Allowing the dark conversation of abortion to enter our minds. Is that belief our true belief? Is taking the life away from an innocent really justifiable? As social constructs and values naturally change over time, does it make them morally right? There are two sides to the argument. One will say that change is necessary and that traditional values become obsolete as time progresses, and the other side believes our fundamental values are what create our successful country. Could our acceptance of these ideas be the psychological effect of preconditioning through a continuous push by the media to make us accept it? Why would they do that? Truly, there should always be a debate between both sides of traditional values versus progressive values. It is healthy to have checks and balances, as there are times in history when progression was the better path or maintaining traditional values was the better path.

Humanity has remained the same throughout history. We will always continue to make the same decisions and mistakes by nature no matter how long into the future we expand. Where there is good, there is evil; where there is darkness, there is light. Regardless if one is evangelical or believes that we were created from evolution, good will always prevail over evil for the greater good as the past continues to repeat itself. As George Santayana once said, "Those who ignore history are doomed to repeat it." There is value in knowing and learning about our previous ancestors and what they had to go through to build what we have at the end of our fingertips today. Generations to come will, by nature, be smarter than their ancestors, but the value of labor will decrease, and generations to come will become ignorant of history and how to write it.

Chapter 9: A Salute to Law Enforcement-Internship Experiences and Other Stories

In my experiences as a student-athlete and entrepreneur, being a criminal justice major was important to further understand human nature and the way temptation can always challenge our free will. In law enforcement, you see everything there is to see. As a police officer or criminal justice major, it eventually comes down to your knowledge that the job entitles the duty of holding more power and responsibility over not just hard-working American citizens but also yourself. With great power comes great responsibility, and in police work, you will have the opportunity to uphold the law or break it just as anyone else. Regardless of what the media may portray about police, there is far less police brutality than what colleges, universities, and high schools are reporting to young tax payers and law-abiding citizens.

In the field of Criminal Law, police are in a position where they will see a variety of different experiences as opposed to what people typically imagine a cop doing. Police are an angelic force who protect and enforce the concepts of justice by definitions of the Constitution, with some who will abuse their position of power and the Constitution. Police are a manifestation of the community they live in. When you're putting your life on the line for the sake of helping rehabilitate and rebuild members of society, this is a holy line of work when most officers simply care about doing their job and getting home to their families. This was my perception of the career during my time as a cop and sheriff's deputy.

Without the police, a society cannot be civil and just. August Volmer, who believed in those same principles, would agree, especially in today's world full of criminals, corrupt politicians, and lawless communities. People often have a distrust towards police through negative experiences, unfair tickets, or damage done to their driving records. It's common to feel more paranoid than protected when a cop passes you by in town. Most press on the brakes and check to see if the cop turns around. In many cases, people tend to dislike the police for pulling them over. But what about if it's somebody driving under the influence? Intoxicated beyond the point of coherency and awareness. At an obvious level of danger to themselves and those around them. If this person you pulled over was your best friend and your partner was with you, what would you honestly do, and what are the potential consequences of that decision? If you decide not to write that ticket, you protect your friendship, but what else? Are you protecting parents and children who may have been driving in the next lane over? Are you sending a positive message of what's right to your best friend and helping them stay out of prison or even a coffin? No, you, of course, wouldn't be.

What about if a police officer breaks up the party that everyone's at? Is there a chance that the same officer who dissolved that party also broke up the chances of an innocent woman or teenager being drugged or raped later that night? Is that a bad cop or a proactive one who sees the potential dangers and only seeks to mitigate the risk of a bad result? Chances personify likelihood in any situation when drugs and alcohol enter into the equation. Officers may be condemned for such action, but the long-term outcome results in a community inevitably being safer. If a cop conforms to the social norms or to the bounds of what a supervisor commands 100% of the time over what the Constitution demands, the cop is committing dereliction of duty and a disservice to his community.

In rebuttal to the argument of police inflicting unnecessary violence at a growing rate, does an intelligent person truly believe the vast majority of law enforcement intends to inflict racism and harm upon the people they encounter? It's usually controversial reasons like these that lead to misconceptions and wrongful perceptions towards law enforcement. Police brutality is as real as the air we breathe. However, the amount of police that represent that statistic accounts for less than 1% of police overall. Police care about the American people and are more concerned with getting home safe to their families before making people's lives harder than they already are.

When I was a senior in high school, our senior class was asked to complete a capstone assignment fulfilling the requirements of reaching at least 10 hours of project work relating to our paper or pertaining to something within the community. I chose to work with my teacher's brother at the time, who was a patrol officer for Detroit City's Eastern Police District. To protect his identity and his work, we will refer to him as officer Matt.

Officer Matt had taken me on the outskirts of 5 Mile to patrol, of course, also in the 8 Mile area near Gratiot in Detroit. When I arrived at the Department, I was escorted through two sets of metal detectors. They took my license and made a copy before giving me a ballistics vest and sending me on my way with Matt.

When job shadowing my senior year of High School, I got to stand inside the burnt-down homes where families once lived on the outskirts of 5 Mile. The first call of that day was an Amber Alert that came across the squad car radio and my phone at the same time. I remember running hot to an arson investigation, a car accident involving death, a carjacking where a driver had a gun to a taxi driver, and even a C-section that followed the car accident. This was all before I had even become a full-time cop and graduated from two consecutive police academies. I'd already seen a lot as just a young kid who hadn't even received a Bachelor's degree yet, but I saw more when I finally became a cop.

After experiencing my ride-along with Detroit City P.D, completing two internships at the sheriff's office I was later hired at, graduating from those two police academies, and eventually getting hired there along with a small city department, I had seen even more crazy things and responded to many more crazy calls. I responded to calls where I had to see the way young teenager finds themselves in a criminal arraignment before they're even old enough to drive a car. I've seen a 17-year-old become paralyzed and brain dead because they didn't wear their seatbelt after drag racing with their friends, striking a tree head-on and breaking their back completely. I've seen many suicides. One where a wealthy middle-aged businessman worth millions, who had everything you could possibly want, shot himself in the face with a .357 magnum, leaving behind a large mansion estate, labradors, speed boats, old classic cars, and his 3 grown children behind. Another was the result of a kid who had committed suicide by shotgun, leaving nothing but his lower body, as the blood spatter covered the walls with bullet splinters scattered across the ceiling, leaving just a letter reading "I'm sorry" behind.

I've seen the way a body turns yellow-green when they are heavily intoxicated or medicated after just a few hours of breathing their last breath. I've seen the way an officer's wife looks into your eyes as her husband is airlifted to the hospital because he has just been shot multiple times. I had seen the look on a woman's face when they were arrested for DUI following the accidental manslaughter of another driver due to her drunkenness. I've seen the way a grown man can be at child-level maturity because of the choice to submit to a life of drugs and narcotics, harming themselves and losing their mind as they could hardly move off the couch due to the toxicity of the substances. I've had to break down a door because the mother thought her daughter had locked herself inside and overdosed. I've given chest compressions at personal injury accidents, only to watch the light go out of a person's eyes and hear the screaming of their friends around them. I've responded to domestics just to see the girlfriend get beaten again and again, only to return to the same home with the boyfriend repeatedly because she was terrified of him.

When compiling those real-life experiences with a college experience forces anyone to see the world through a different lens. You learn to be careful, aware of your surroundings, and practice good ethics daily, as police work is a profession that allows for few errors. Lawsuits are becoming a daily enemy to fear; aside from a world of cameras surrounding the officer's every move, it is enough of an extra weight on an officer's shoulders.

Becoming a police officer and witnessing a body in rigor-mortis and knowing that person was your neighbor just 12 hours ago creates a better understanding of death and why life is so important to embrace. You begin to recognize what's important over the exchangeable commodity of money or lustful desires for popularity and perfection. Seeing enough darkness has a way of magnifying the light. You naturally evolve into placing others above yourself, which in return, develops character and leadership if you are self-aware and intentional about making a difference for the better. The drive of a man who has nothing to lose and everything to gain is stronger than a man who has everything to lose and nothing to gain. The same goes for a police officer, firefighter, combat veteran, or doctor. In any line of work where your career is to see what human eyes are not meant to or witness the most terrifying of occurrences, a sense of clarity falls over what is important in life. A soldier who witnesses both good and evil becomes the general who inevitably will combat evil to defend what is good. Until you've seen it, you may never believe it. Until you've experienced the ground, you'll never be able to climb the mountain. In any profession that involves risking one's life or saving another, it involves the sacrifice of self-concern and your own personal gain. People walking around you become more precious, and each breath you breathe becomes more appreciated and valuable.

In June of 2019, three years after my experiences with Detroit City Police Department, I spent my first internship at the County Sheriff's Department, where I witnessed the autopsy of a man we will call Roger for respect for his real identity. In the autopsy, we learned how Roger had died and what others had said about him before his death. It was a strange coincidence that my cousin had been working as a cop in the same county, so he was with me during this autopsy. He was working as a city officer, and I was interning with the county sheriff's detective bureau that week. Roger had been drinking before passing out and drowning in the Flint River. During my internship is when I got to be inside the room during the autopsy. I remember seeing his discolored body being pulled out of the bodybag and placed on the table for the forensic pathologist to properly conduct his work. Because he had been dead for 2 weeks, he was a greenish color from the water, and it was hard to even make out his face from the deterioration. He was 5'7" with a bit of hair still attached to his cranium and a tattoo on his right leg that read 'Maria.' I wondered what had happened to Maria and whether she was in his life at the time of his death. What would she do if she were in the position I was in, seeing his body in the state it was in? Did she have anything to do with his death? I wondered who Maria was and what she meant to the man, as we were only given a handful of information and could not accurately make out his face. I remember wondering what his last thought was before dying. As I saw the pathologist at work, I wondered if the man's soul was somewhere else. I wondered if it was in another dimension or if he was simply meant to see God on the day of his last heartbeat. I wondered what he was looking forward to in the next week and where he had been previously. We learned the man was liked by everybody and had very few enemies. Due to intoxication, he passed out in the Flint River and ingested high amounts of water into the nasal cavity. This gave the pathologist and medical examiner reason to believe he was struggling to stand up and was trying to breath underwater.

I will never forget that autopsy. It was the beginning of my career in the criminal justice field and the beginning of transitioning from childhood to adulthood. Instantly, that moment required maturity and maintaining a sense of urgency. I prayed more after that day. Not because I was afraid of death or the reality of this career, but because I knew how important it was to do so regularly just in case my time had expired on Earth for some freak occurrence.

There are many more calls I responded to as a police officer, as well as trials that I've sat through. I've witnessed a trial of a man who was arrested for D.U.I., who had crashed his vehicle after driving over 100 mph with his girlfriend and babies in the vehicle at the time of the crash. It was a miracle that everyone survived. I remember the way a girlfriend cried when she testified, solidifying her spouse's next 10 years in prison. The way they looked at each other in the room, both knowing his life was over.

I remember seeing the Deputy on the scene, who is now a Sergeant for that department, being questioned on the stand and crying himself just because of how shocking and wicked the crime was. He testified as to how he, too, had children and how he struggled to save the defendant's baby as the vehicle was totaled and flipped at the scene. I remember watching the jury's reaction and seeing the way their facial expressions changed as the facts slowly unraveled. It was an eye-opening experience as a future cop who was still trying to get his degree and get a starting spot on his college football team. I had seen the way the real world operated and how life really was, not just how my college professors made it all seem. I experienced many other stories like this one, and it made me a man. Thank God for great deputies and officers like the ones I learned from.

Chapter 10: Networking: Building Connections

Alexander the Great was one of the most brilliant thinkers of his time and one of the most brilliant rulers of Persia and Macedonia in 336 B.C. He never lost a single battle because he was a genius military leader. He once said, "There is nothing impossible to him who will try." He was able to rule his empire because of this mentality. Don't be afraid to take the risks of going to college or starting a business. Go as far as you can. The most important thing about the working world, or especially college, whether you're trying to get into one, whether you're in one, or whether you're graduating from one, is networking.

Making connections is perhaps the most essential component of building any long-lasting brand, getting an internship, scoring points with a recruiter or coach, making/keeping friends, landing a concrete position in the workplace, and successfully receiving your official degree on graduation day, and quite literally, in life when it comes down to it. The United States government has always had an act for gaining and keeping close "friends" or "allies" in order to fulfill the agenda of American dominance, which is to hold global power and independence, as any great nation strives to do. Likewise, you have to be intentional about going out of your way to make new connections every day so your long-term agenda can be met if you're trying to reach levels of the 1%.

For example, the famous antagonist from The Walking Dead, Neagan, said in one episode, "Every person is a resource." This was always one of my favorite quotes from the show because it is absolutely a fact. Every single person has unique qualities and gifts inside of them. Abilities and qualities that are difficult to replicate. Certain personality types, natures, certain swaggers, and certain skill sets are what make each person individually and totally unique - even if they themselves don't know it. People have the ability to speak, save you time, and help you get to the completion point of any objective. People have ideas and experiences you can always learn from and use to your own advantage. People have connections, and they can teach you their ways if they are successful in what they do best. Every word another person says is a word that could provide meaning and purpose to your life and to your successful future. As no penny is wasted currency, no person speaks a worthless word.

When I was a junior going into my senior year in high school, I learned quickly that in order to ever be able to call yourself a collegiate student-athlete, attending college visits, and putting yourself out there was the only way to find yourself on a college football or baseball field chasing a degree at the same time. Shaking hands, making the drives, sending emails, making phone calls, being the standout in small groups at events, asking for help, and sucking up your pride is the game of success in all things. Making personal, meaningful, valuable, and long-lasting relationships are what catapults you further than your competition. As my high school football coach used to say, " a handshake goes a long way."

You must guard your success like a Lion guarding his meal. Success is easily lost by carelessness and the illusion of trust and progress. With just a bit of laziness, drifting, procrastination, outdated information, and lack of focus, you can easily find yourself losing grasp of your accomplishments and how you define "success." College is full of followers and full of deceivers, just as in business or any aspect of life. Leaders are not afraid to be stingy about their connections and be sturdy when meeting and learning the patterns of each new person they meet. This is the psychology of networking. You have to have something to offer. You need to validate yourself while also validating the other person. You have to be willing to spend money to make new connections if you want to compound your reach and maximize attention. Make dear, sincere, and close friends with all, but trust few. Mastering makes you the master of your own destiny in any situation, which later will bring confidence in first impressions and certainty with each judgment of character.

A great example of great networkers is those who benefited from the criminological study of social bonding theory, founded by Hirschi in 1969. Those who apply it in their everyday lives socially are often those who find themselves at the center of the world - television, news media, and social media. People who operate in social bonding theory also tend to avoid being outcasted or in trouble with the law, as their connections to different networks create security based on relationships and, you guessed it - bonds. A person who is big on television or social media today has likely studied the arts of networking and social bond theory. They must be committed to a purpose, they must be a known person in the community, and their beliefs have to "conform" to a society based on that person's intent for generating mass Influence. The elements of one who engages in social bond theory are as follows: attachment, commitment, involvement, and belief.

Powerful executives and CEOs who have infinite wealth and influence, or in other words, people who hold all the cards, are the ones who decide who gets to be seen and heard based on their attachment, commitment, involvement, and belief. It doesn't matter if you're Donald Trump, Barack Obama, Kim Kardashian, Lebron James, Jimmy Fallon, Blake Shelton, or even just a stranger who's on the news. National television and press attention derive from meeting those four elements of social attachment, commitment, involvement, and belief within the walls of social bonding. Control theory is a synonymous term with social bonding theory, and without being a practitioner of those communicative arts, you can never create mass Influence in life, and you can never truly connect or relate to society. In the world of social media, it isn't different. Compiling these elements together makes one significantly more popular, powerful, and seen by the eye - giving those people massive Influence, reach, bandwidth, economic flexibility, a clean criminal record (in most cases), power, and social confidence. Social bonding theory is an important theory to advocate if you're trying to be known and socially relatable to the environment, connected to the rule of law simultaneously. It is a big part of networking and making connections.

Chapter 11: Relationships - The Golden Rule, Long Distance, Trust, & Due Diligence

Relationships are a risk for a person chasing total success in one's self because a relationship requires your time and full attention. A long-lasting relationship requires the classic Golden Rule taught in elementary school, "Treat others the way you want to be treated." Like anything you love, it requires passion and good timing. It requires due diligence and respect. You have to be careful about dating when you're young and about to go to college. When college becomes a way of life, it threatens the stability of a relationship if long-distance becomes a reality. With a relationship, you sacrifice time, independence, control, money, priorities, goals, and sometimes even dreams for the sake of somebody else's happiness. With a relationship, you also can gain something as rare as trust and companionship, so you have to make the decision of what's most important to you - love or individual success. A relationship is something many people can't manage to even find, so when one comes along, you shouldn't waste the opportunity. The hard part is spotting the right person and making the right choice as to whether or not they are a good fit for you in the long term. Just be cautious and remain your own self, and never become selfish.

Practice due diligence in the arena of love, as it is a vicious and dangerous battlefield.

Going into college, high school relationships rarely work out in the end, and it's something to warn people about. It's nobody's fault. It's just the way the world works. Long distance relationships never work, and I've not only experienced it, but I've seen the result of them with friends and family. I've seen the result of people giving their hearts and soul only to be crushed because they didn't guard their hearts enough. Trust is absent. Communication and physical touch matter and long distance will only collapse if that is absent too. It's not a means of pessimism but simply an obstacle of realism to endure. As such, respect is equally important. Love has to be mutual, and if it isn't, move on to the next fish in the sea of 7.7 billion people. A relationship can create an alternate timeline, and if you fall into one, you will share the future of that person. So ask yourself, where are they heading in the future, and do you want to be there?

The experience of sharing something intimate is unlike anything you could read in this book. The feeling of waking up next to the love of your life as her eyes stay closed in peace is truly sacred. People look and act their best every day, specifically to find just that. Her skin touches yours, and you can hear the blood rushing in her head, her heart beating, as she sleeps on your chest - that is peace. You protect her universe, and you ask yourself why you even deserve such a perfect being. Even though being single opens the doors for opportunity and individual success, there is no greater joy than love and intimacy. Love and intimacy keep us alive. It keeps us human and willing to be our best selves. We need human connection, and we need physical affection to make us complete.

One of the basic necessities of life is love. A relationship makes a person selfless and turns them into a caregiver. But with love still comes foolishness and complacency. With love comes both greatness and disaster. With love comes both blinding perspectives and clarity all at once. Even if a relationship is so horrible that it changes your life in ways you never expected, you will always have good memories, and your shortcomings will always stay with you as lessons for the future. It's your decision to make the most of every experience and pursue the happiness that comes with love. As once said by British author Alfred Lord Tennyson, "It's better to have loved and lost than to have never loved at all." A relationship may conflict with your individual success, but love is a rarity that should always be embraced when presented. Love happens for a reason, and love is something to celebrate and hold dear.

You should always be diligent about who you choose to date, as it's important when you have eyes on getting a college degree or achieving your desired outcome of any sort. It's important whether you're 16 years old or 96 years old. College requires focus and commitment, and distractions threaten to focus more than anything. Relationships are a distraction when you do them right. Getting into college requires maintaining a good reputation, and a relationship in high school can make or break that. Relationships come easy when you're a big bad senior with a good reputation, but the way you treat a girl will reflect on you overall. If you go through a dirty high school breakup, pray your ex never has dirt on you because they will expose it. If you send the wrong texts, say the wrong words, or do the wrong things, your reputation becomes damaged by your actions and can lead to a rejection of a college application. More so, your decisions early on can affect your ability to get a good job or take a certain path. Male or female, whoever you date will take a role in impacting your future, especially if you're both seniors applying to go to schools three and a half hours away from each other. This can be a disaster waiting to happen. It's one of the most important things to remember when seeking to graduate college with a clear mind, clear focus, and clear intent.

One of the most detrimental moves you can make as a senior trying to get into college is to carry the weight of a girlfriend/boyfriend on your back when they're planning on going to a school hours away from you. Long distance is a deal breaker. It's the hardest thing to break off a relationship early because of something like long distance, but it's the best move you can make considering the alternatives and long-term benefits. In college, you meet people. Your significant other will be surrounded by new people, frat houses, parties, dances, and opportunities, just as you will be. You're constantly around new people, and as time goes on with new changes, feelings can change. In a long-distance relationship, communication becomes limited to FaceTime and hanging out every other week if excuses don't arise by week two. Women love intimacy and connection. Men love the same. When intimacy and connection are absent, coupled with temptations, feelings can change quickly. In a long-distance relationship, if you don't have trust, the relationship is as good as dead, and I can't oversell the point enough.

Every person should be important to you, and the ones you date speak volumes about who you are and what you believe in. There are 7.7 billion people on planet Earth. Every experience should be an opportunity to learn about the interests of the person across from you. Get inside their brains. In high school and throughout my time in college, I dated girls who were outgoing, honest, hard-working, and unique from the crowd because I was able to learn about who they were and what they cared about. I learned about their struggles. I listened. I was seen as a player, but I always laughed because it was never true. I loved love, and I learned to be selective. Even in the dating world, you have to be selfish for yourself, and you have to guard your heart in a world of hopeless romantics. As enticing as love can be, your future will be affected by your vulnerability. Love is a privilege, and it must be guarded and cherished when it comes and goes. Your own blindness to the dangers of love can make you a victim of heartbreak and poor judgment, so stay vigilant and be wise about what you want in life. Know where you want to be. For the sake of being classy, know what you want with an open mind.

I've seen close friends, family, and some of the most famous people in the world lose their lives from choosing love without due diligence. I've seen family and friends struggle from failing to get prenuptial agreements, which protect your assets in the case of a divorce. My Uncle, who was a car hauler for Jack Cooper's Trucking, was nearly a multi-millionaire in his mid 40's. He owned an exquisite home in Lapeer County, Michigan, and had two children who worked closely in the Criminal Justice field. My uncle was a good-looking, 6'1, blue-collar trucker who loved cracking jokes and drinking beer aside from building things in his barn. A charming, blue-collar, do-it-yourself kind of guy with charisma and laughter every time you saw him.

When he met this woman he had only known for six months, he married her, and they later divorced.

My Uncle's ex-wife was the reason his bank account dropped significantly by what seemed like thousands every month. Our entire family felt horrible for him. She sold life insurance for a living and had a hobby for bodybuilding, leaching off of my Uncle for more and more money until he nearly killed himself trying to make her happy - only so she could cheat on him and break his heart. My Uncle chose unwisely, and he married a woman he should have never married, as so many people do. More importantly, he married a woman he couldn't trust. My Uncle failed to get a prenuptial agreement and, sadly, never knew who he was marrying. His assets took a major hit all because he couldn't see the deception in front of his eyes. His children (my cousins) resented his failure to know what was good for him until he finally paid the harsher price of divorce when it was too late. When he finally divorced her, he was able to save his money again, and he later met somebody he could trust, but his failure to have due diligence and trust destroyed his marriage and could have made him poor. He was used, and his family, along with himself, was hurt in the process. We can't control how the ones we love change, but we have to have due diligence when a relationship is no longer able to grow. We have to have a sense of urgency and be wise about how a relationship can change who we are, whether it be in better ways or worse. A relationship can decide your future if you're not self-aware.

To me, there was a great intrigue about girls who had their own way of thinking. If I was ever going to date, she was going to be somebody who shared my personality and long-term goals. I liked choosing girls who had goals and motivation. Free spirits were always the most attractive, with a passion for being independent. I found beauty in women who made everything out of life and out of every experience. If I met a girl who was different from me, I took time to learn about who she was and why she thought differently. In relationships, you have to make them a priority, and you have to put the person on your list of things to tend to because a strong relationship requires work in order to make it work.

The Golden Rule is the most important thing in any relationship aside from trust and honesty. "Treat others the way you would like to be treated" goes a long way in life. The power of having due diligence can save your life in any relationship, and it can save the troubles of long distances in college, which only lead to failure. Love is a privilege, and it must be guarded like a sacred scroll. You must watch everyone like a hawk so they don't try to derail your success. Love is full of temptations and unexpected emotions, full of uncertainty. Love is a blessing, but love can make one a fool if they don't understand the nature of love and these basic fundamentals. Love is dangerous if you fall too hard. You have to be somewhat selfish, and you have to put yourself first at the end of the day.

Whether male or female, relationships require attention and making sacrifices. Whoever you are with in college is who you could likely share a future with. Do you want the same future? Can you trust that person with your life? Is there baggage in the relationship? Can the relationship affect your future? Can the relationship last? Can the relationship grow? Are you happy? Those are the key questions to answer. You have to be wise enough to choose your partners with a very careful selection. The person you choose to spend the rest of your life with and have children with matters because they are essentially the mate you are choosing to spread your genes with. What do you want your children to be like physically and mentally? Be careful who you choose as your life partner.

Chapter 12: 24 House: Engineering Your Schedule

There are 24 hours in a day. It's been a famous quote used by Arnold Schwarzenegger, Sylvester Stallone, and so many other famous minds. It was famously said, "There are only 24 hours in a day. The average man has to sleep about 8 hours. And work for 8 hours. That leaves 8 hours to run some errands, drive to and from work, eat, and have some spare time. And in that little bit of spare time, a man has to figure out how to get the one thing he likes more than anything else: sex." The feeling of sex is the one thing every person inherently strives to get ever since human beings were primates. There's a social trophy statement about being with somebody who's strong, confident, and successful in terms of both financial status and persona. Success is the archetype of passion and standards, all too relatable to the results of organizing your time accordingly in your own 24 hours so that you can get that one thing we all care for so deeply, which is indeed that same feeling of sex - Success.

Those who can manage their time can manage their goals. These are the leaders in the world. You must be able to manage your time in college if you ever want that trophy statement form of living when you're 30 years old and at the age of raising your first kids. It's a natural desire to be perceived as the alpha male or female who can have whoever he or she wants due to their Success and confidence in life. It's an unspoken truth. The feeling of orgasm and great emotional high keeps us going and competing for the best-looking woman or man - the alpha. We strive to be the alphas of our own world when we're motivated and in the right state of mind.

When you wake up, you have the time, no matter how many different tasks you can be doing. Period. There are no excuses for time because you only get one lifetime to make your name one of historical significance. There is no time to waste. If a lawyer who works 60 to 80 hours a week can do it, then you can do it. If a single mom can do it, then you can do it. If Elon Musk, Jeff Bezos, and Richard Branson were able to accomplish the many brilliant things they did all at once while handling billions and managing hundreds of thousands of employees a day, then you can do it too. It only takes an empowered imagination and an intentional spirit to Succeed - a willingness to commit everything you have towards the Greatness of tomorrow's future. It only takes desire and intention. There must be a passionate motivation for growth and problem-solving, and if you don't like those things - learn to like them, or you'll drown in this primal universe we call life. When you have those pieces to the puzzle, the ideas come together all of a sudden.

When you wake up in the morning to get up for work, usually everything becomes very routine after a period of time because it works for you. It benefits you to do things in a certain way, and if it works, never change something that isn't broken. But the milliseconds you have every day are often unnoticeably taken for granted, and you are to blame. It's often people do things without accepting that they're not using every second of the day to their best advantage, and for many, it can really destroy and eviscerate somebody's self-esteem, confidence, mojo, and competitive drive. For example, video games and the screen time spent on Instagram, Twitter, and Facebook. The hours spent watching Netflix and racking up contacts on Snapchat and Tinder. The time spent partying, planning, talking, pondering, complaining, second-guessing, and dreaming rather than doing. Imagining rather than implementing those thoughts and emotions into one physical presentation, one masterpiece, a work of art, or some type of service. Squandering those gifts becomes our greatest shackles that weigh us down like a docked ship, never setting sail to voyage and discover the unknown. It's not a lack of understanding to me, but rather an intentional choice not to do those things outside of what can build a better future for my Grandchildren's Grandchildren. Time is of the essence, and you have your entire life to sleep and ponder, but you don't have your entire life to become everything you've ever wanted. Never be a person filled with regrets. It's never too late to accomplish your destiny.

I would rather be diligent with my own time and pursue the knowledge it takes to climb the ladder and leave a legacy of honorable and Influential works. I never found joy in wasting my early life partying, although I had fun with friends and college peers on more than enough occasions. What brought me unrest was how I was making that choice myself to never apply attention to all the magnificent things that can be done with a sober mind. It was my decision to spend that time doing less important things for the next generation, and it ate me all the time. I hated not focusing on my goals when I knew there were other people hustling and climbing that ladder to achieve their dreams.

I have always been a hard worker because I am aware that the 1% are out there busting ass to beat me and become their very best. Every second wasted is a second well spent by your competition. Even though there is nothing wrong with partying and enjoying the finer memories and moments in life, which is also a gateway to meeting new people and networking, I've always lived inside of my own head and followed the lead of engineering my schedule so that I am the master of my own universe at the end of the day. This is my own way of operating, and it's how I was able to make it through college, sports, work, start businesses, and establish my writing career all at once. Choosing to take action and work when you'd rather sleep, and if you choose to open your mind to new and intriguing ideas, those ideas can manifest themselves into true realities. You only need to take action and pull the trigger on those ideas. Dreams can absolutely become true, and you have to keep looking towards the stars, never failing to remember that you live in a universe full of infinite possibilities. It only requires you to do it, walk-the-walk, and be diligent about how you spend your time.

There should be a balance of goal setting, saving money, taking action on those goals, spending time with family, spending time with friends, reading to enhance your knowledge, staying in physical shape, and networking whenever you can. Make sure your word is always your bond, and never fail to match your actions with your words. If you lie, take responsibility and be the first to expose your lies and make the truth clear. Say what you feel, and do what is necessary to Succeed while being maliciously intentional and industrious. As Jesus Christ once said in his own words to the 12 disciples in Matthew 10:16, " I am sending you out like sheep among wolves. So, therefore, be as shrewd as snakes and as innocent as doves." Be inside of people's minds every second of the day, let them speak and do what they do, while in your own reality, you are pursuing goals and accomplishing micro task after micro task, climbing your golden ladder to the heights of your envisioned Success. Never back down to the naysayers and the people who are wrapped in bondage and doubt.

When you wake up and go to work, let's say a 9-5 work day, you get back home, and you're exhausted. Let's say college, where the schedule can be scattered and unpredictable, you have a job to do. You're physically and mentally exhausted every day, and the very thought of further mental effort makes the headache pound harder.

When you're in college, it's class after class, family worries, anxiety over who your boyfriend/girlfriend is talking to when you're not around, and you're thinking about the future carefully, with uncertainty very often among the average majority of the public. College is a test of your mental strength and your ability to finish what you start while being surrounded by thousands who differ from your own beliefs. I've found it a part of my natural lifestyle to count the minutes, the seconds in my head after first completing my first semester of Freshman year in college. I became an amateur journalist by being a Criminal Justice major because I was constantly writing criminal profile reports and compiling projects, group assignments, and essays, all due by a deadline. There were no exceptions at Olivet College. Timing always had to be right, and late work was marked a zero.

In both football and baseball, you had to know how to manage your time. Yet I was admittedly always more perplexed by those who chose to use their spare time for creative works.

When the kids are asleep, and when you only have 3 hours before work starts again, you do have the choice to use those 3 hours to build your own system of income, whatever it may be, and to use your imagination to formulate an alternative path (a plan B path to rely on if you were to lose your primary career). You should always be building and adding onto ways in which you can generate solid, stable net income so you can live a quality and financially Independent life. And, of course, these should be in multiple forms of income.

I had friends in high school who were tremendous artists, smart, talented, gifted people. They could have easily done things like draw and sell album covers, craft and sell paintings, sculpt statues for celebrities, sing on American Idol, or sell their music on Spotify, but they never did, and it was sad to me. They didn't use that extra time, even if it was one hour a night, to pursue their childhood dreams and make it a business when they had the talent to do it. They didn't make their room, their dorm, their office.

I was surprised why so many kids I had grown up with never tried to build their own brands or dedicate their time to creative masterpieces, which would've helped them write their name in the history books or at least die trying. "How can people not spend hours in silence reading and planning for their futures in a world that has such little predictability?" I always thought to myself. I was curious to see what would happen if I used my time more wisely every day and spent it on doing research. Spending hours of smartphone and sleep time studying psychology, philosophy, sociology, geopolitics, and criminal social and scientific behavior while getting my Bachelor's degree. When I woke up, I'd go to my classes, do homework, perfect my side hustles, go to practice for football and baseball, return to my dorm, then I would spend up to at least 4 hours doing research on how to perfect my crafts, totally isolating myself, just reading and learning how to build my own brand so I could one day build a home for my Mother and Grandmother. I made my dorm my office. Instead of partying and doing what everyone else did in college, I was learning how to start businesses and build systems. I would get maybe an hour or two of sleep because I was always hustling, trying to make something of my life - I wasted little time. But that doesn't mean I was never having fun.

I enjoyed long nights making those important memories with football friends as well, drinking, listening to Post

Malone, talking about exes, speaking nonsense, and acting like we knew everything; I had fun, and I had my days of drinking and wasting time as well. We were never shy of going after the best-looking women on our campus and discussing the most important topics of the 21st century all at once. I was always working on political manuscripts to perfect as I took an interest in the state of America's affairs. But even in accomplishing many goals, college has to be a time of fun too, and if you don't put in a little time to have fun in your schedule, you'll collapse and burn out. You'll drift away from your goals like a ship with no anchor. You'll coast away from your dreams like a lost soul without a compass. Allow yourself to get an hour of peace of mind, plan diligently, make memories, succeed regularly, and refuse to fail permanently. Stay focused.

I really valued the lessons I learned in college, and I absorbed how to be an attention-to-detail entrepreneur over those 4 years in getting my Bachelor's Degree. I learned how to avoid being a robot who conformed to every word my professors said. I have always been more of a contrarian. I never agreed with using my own precious time to craft my own thoughts and ideas just so that a room of conformists who had no true courage to speak or stand out from the crowd could lecture me on how I needed to agree with whatever the professor told me to be true. I always wanted to know the source of the information that I was supposed to just "believe" without question. I liked being the brave one who had the balls to speak and state my case, even if I was wrong. There is nobility and respect owed to a person who can express organic and original thoughts and ideas.

College is all about conformity. Giving in to conformity is the ultimate waste of precious time because you're squandering time that could be put into perfecting your greater interests. Conformity in a college classroom looks like a bunch of people who never say anything, never ask pressing questions, always agree to the narrative of the professor, and shame anyone who doesn't think the same as them. There is, quite frankly, biblical and evolutionary reasoning behind why human beings behave that way, but it's only damaging to what we can truly be and manifest if you're playing the long game in life. What human beings can do is far beyond the limitations that any professor will require you to abide by in order for you to pass the class.

It's not easy to survive college. It's a game, just like life. It's a contest to see who has the tolerance, the grit, the will, the vision, and the well-mastered art of patience. You're surrounded by people totally different from you, and it can be hard to tolerate and respect, but if you can respect it, you will find yourself soaring in college and outlasting most of the Freshmen you were with 4 years ago. Completing college is a lifelong reward in itself because it can never be taken away from you, and it's an instant salary bonus if you can get the degree (so long as you find a career you like that generates good income). An instant character bonus comes from the accomplishment itself. You're perceived as somebody who is an expert beyond the levels of one who only holds a High School Diploma and is seen as a sure thing. You are seen as reliable, dependable, and trustworthy. That is something to be proud of. However, your time can never be wasted on conforming to a classroom that doesn't share your same goals, foresight, mindset, life experiences, or imagination. This will slaughter every dream you have, and it will make you full of resentment. Be bold in college and be your own individual, never one who conforms just to be cool or fit-in. What you can accomplish is never based on what a classroom tells you is possible. What you can accomplish is based on how you engineer your time, focus, work ethic, vision, and networking capabilities. All of those together can make Glorious things happen.

When you are enduring those frustrating parts of college, like the time spent debating controversial issues, fighting with your significant other, working, studying, procrastinating, dealing with family issues, and being surrounded by people opposite to you - this will always be important because in college you have to play the long game and you have to play it with the intention to finish, having an open mind to all ideas so you can better your own scope of knowledge and expertise. How do you presume most Congress representatives are able to sit and tolerate their opposing party completely ripping apart their beliefs and views, despite their differing views? They learned patience and the art of tolerance. They spent enough time reading and learning so that they always had something to pull out of their back pocket. That is time well spent in college, and your degree will overshadow that.

What makes people see college students as brilliant critical thinkers in society is their ability to think critically and not be afraid to do so independently without their peers making them enemies of the overall group. The ability to speak and address your opinions to trade thoughts and ideas, never to conform to a system where a professor tells you otherwise, is how college should be. Where ideas and passion can flow freely. The sad part is that in 2020, when this portion of this book was written, America's Freedom of Speech was nearly taken away in colleges and universities. As I write and edit this book today, in 2023, nothing has changed. In fact, it has gotten even worse. Even expressing different ideas and narratives outside of the collective academic consortiums would make you seem like a lost lunatic to students who were largely just bobble heads to whatever a professor would say, never questioning a single claim or source. It isn't to say that your professors know nothing, but we all know nothing, and it's better we remember that inherently with each generation than act like we know everything. Experience can only take one so far, but ideas are priceless and deserve to be expressed freely without silencing the conversation, to begin with.

    In the next 5 decades, we will likely see the numbers in homeschooling and trade schools go up while attendance at government-funded universities will go down unless Free Speech is protected within the walls of mainline academia. Conformity is death to free thought and ideas. Conforming makes every person less individual and more concerned about society's view of them rather than making their ideas and thoughts heard so that they can be useful assets to society. It's why social media is filled with scared people who develop mental illnesses over how many likes a post gets. People post because they want to be liked and seen, potentially in with the crowd of celebrities and lavish billionaires. People want to be just as, or cooler, than their rival best friends, able to feel cared for and appreciated through the illusion of a glass screen that only wastes essential time that could be used to build your brand, your masterpiece, passive income, or whatever it may be. Unless social media is the way of building that brand or masterpiece specifically, for most people, their time could be better spent making comic books, music, memoirs, manuscripts, and building their own source of income. Being self-made requires the sacrifice of doing things that are fun in the short term. Life is all about fun, but to me, fun is when you can be financially free, educated with a degree, and able to go anywhere at any time, able to look at the hard work and the sacrifices you've made and say "Wow - I fucking made it."

In college, I learned how to be a learner, an earner, and a leader. I learned to handle the terrifying word "no" and manage my own time so that I could one day be of service to 8 billion other people's time. Time is one luxury that should never be wasted when human beings have an expiration date. Engineering my own time became an important and critical part of building things like essays, social media networks, YouTube channels, my books, screenplays, websites, powerpoints, podcasts, a good grade point average, a career in Criminal Justice, and a respected reputation overall throughout my lifetime.

Time is absolutely priceless, and it should be closely monitored to be sure that we are doing everything we can to live a forward-moving life full of accomplishment and make our dreams become manifested realities. It can be done with intention and attention to your own schedule. The timeline you are in now should never be taken for granted. Be an engineer of how you manage your time because it will decide how much time you have left to do things you never got to do when time is running out later. While we're on planet Earth, time is limited, and it comes down to 24 hours. How are you going to change the world in that 24 hours? How wisely will you spend your time in that 24 hours? What can you build today? Whose life could you save? How many goals can you accomplish? Imagine the ways you could change the world if you thought about it and planned for it 24 hours a day with all of your mind and focus.

Chapter 13: Dodging the Freshman Fifteen: Maintaining Physical Balance

There's a known archetype that when you go to college, it's just natural to gain fifteen pounds from drinking, partying, breaking up with high school sweethearts, eating good snacks you fill in the mini refrigerator, and sleeping so much that you miss the necessary workouts you need to stay in shape. This is known as the freshman fifteen. But don't go down that route. If you have, you can always make a comeback and change your life. When you get to college, you'll have a thousand excuses to gain the freshman fifteen and add a few pounds. You'll want to justify not being able to fit your varsity jacket from High School at the five-year reunion by saying you went through hard times or drank too many beers. You'll be on the fence, and the men will say that girls like a dad bod more anyways. Well, if that makes you happy, then go for it. To some, staying in shape physically simply isn't that important. You'll certainly find that not every Successful person who lived looked like Zac Effron or Chris Hemsworth. But it does make life more pleasurable to hold yourself to those standards, and it will, without a doubt, make you a happier person.

Dodging the freshman fifteen is a challenge that should always be promoted rather than avoided. If your physical body is in shape and in healthy condition, fueled by a healthy diet and workout routine, you'll feel better mentally in the real world, and you'll be able to walk with that much more confidence. It's important that you stay in shape and keep a healthy lifestyle because if you want to change the world, you have to try and stick around for a long time, and staying in shape physically will help you live a longer life 9 times out of 10. Granted, it's not out of understanding to me that some struggle with it. We're all created with different genetic makeups, and some have it easier than others growing up. There are many who are born out of heavier-set families and many who are born out of lighter-set families. These things are true, and they come into play when it comes to your devotion to weight loss and exercise, but there is still the ability to change that course and change the way you look. You can change your family bloodline. You have the ability to lose a hundred pounds or gain a hundred pounds if your mind is set on the task enough. You have to want it, and for some, it takes digging deep in order for them to build the motivation to pursue it continuously. But it is possible.

The reason I take staying in shape, so personally is because working out releases endorphins, and it gives your body a dopamine rush. Working out can be like taking the hardest drug, except working out is great for your body. When you do any type of cardiovascular exercise that makes you sweat and pump oxygen to the brain, your body will trigger a chemical reaction, and you'll almost get high off of the effects. When you sprint across a 100-yard football field and back, you're pumping blood to the brain and releasing those endorphins, and your body will sweat out the toxic chemicals. When you finish a set of 12 repetitions on the bench press at just 50% of your own body weight, your muscles will thank you, and they'll stimulate and contract, thus transforming your body into what you want it to look like the more you repeat the cycle. Working out is essential for your brain to function, your body to function, and most importantly, your mind to function. You can become something that you never thought possible, and no matter what the rest of the pack says, you will have the work ethic and the realization that you look better than the pack because you worked your body harder. There is no shame in the dad bod, but the ability to go above and beyond will be far more worth it later.

I was lucky in college because my freshman year consisted of excruciating workouts and hours of taking a beating at football and baseball practices. Six hours of nothing but clashing shoulder pads in 95-degree weather is bound to make anyone look better than they did before. We had a former marine as our strength and conditioning coach who used to fight on the UFC (Ultimate Fighting Championship) Mayweather card. He was an MMA stallion and intimidating to the core. He was 5'11 with about 230 pounds of solid muscle and total flexibility, able to kick anybody's ass. He kept "The Art of War" in his main office at Olivet College before he moved on to bigger things in his career. His nickname was "True Grit," and he forced all weakness out of those who had the will to make it through his workouts. He later became my boss when I got the job to be Olivet's weight room supervisor at the Cutler.

True Grit was always about winning, and he meant business. If you didn't do it right, you'd do it again. If you couldn't run a lap around the track of the game field within a minute and forty seconds, you'd run it again. He was the hardcore Navy Seal/SWCC drill instructor type. Do it right the first time, or do it again until it's right, despite how tired you'd be in running the previous lap. In the weight room, he'd hit the punching bag, and it'd feel like it was shaking the building. True Grit was a man who knew anything was possible. He had been to Hell and back during his time in the Marine Corps, and his mindset was strong as an ox, and this is why he was able to look the way he did and motivate those around him. He was committed and dedicated to perfecting his body and mind - pushing them to their limits. If you want to look good and avoid the freshman fifteen, you have to think like True Grit.

Dwayne "The Rock" Johnson is famous for his career in WWE and acting, but more importantly, his massive physical presence and will to Succeed. But if you study his mind and his will to Succeed, you'll learn that his body never magically became covered in muscles overnight. Dwayne Johnson works out 6 hours a day, every day, and he's done it consistently his entire life, even when having only 7 dollars in his bank account. If you were to ask him how he did it, he wouldn't say it just happened from hard work and time in the weight room. It would go deeper than that. He'd tell you, "Success isn't always about 'Greatness. 'It's about consistency. Consistent, hard work gains success. Greatness will come." Success and making your body look to your liking requires passion to make it happen. Consistency is the key to making any fine art a lifestyle. Without this philosophy, you'll never truly be the best in anything, and you'll often let yourself down. Be amazing, and push against the tides of the universe if you want to see beyond the horizon.

Chapter 14: Proving Them Wrong - Patience and Process

I changed my life 180 degrees the day my high school world history teacher told me my signature would be worth something someday. This teacher was a graduate of Michigan State University and extremely bright. He loved every one of his students, and he would cover the walls with historical newspaper clippings and always wore MSU fan gear with khakis. He was one of the few teachers who truly deserved a plaque on the wall because of his devotion to helping the lives of his students with absolute intention, as he never gave up on even the worst Apple schools have to offer. Although our political affiliations were opposite, we got along well and listened to one another's points of view. I was more of a Conservative-minded student, while he was a Liberal-minded teacher, as most tend to be. But this didn't matter. We would often discuss important topics about race, socioeconomic differences, world issues, and changing culture, and we would listen to what one another had to say. We had many discussions that truly left a mark on both of our lives. However, there was one day in particular that was a defining moment in my life.

I was sitting in class, finishing an assignment, turning in my paper, and as always, I wrote my signature in the name/date portion of the assignment. One sentence changed my entire work ethic, and it planted a seed for me to exceed all expectations and reach for the stars. I remember that sentence every day. He looked at my paper, impressed by the signature, and said, "Is this your signature, Brendan?" I replied, "Yes," only hearing him say these few words, "Wow. Could be worth something someday". It was nothing more than that, nothing too big, but it gave me absolute drive, and I felt that I suddenly had a responsibility to uphold that potential possibility of being that guy who could make his signature worth something. This was the day I learned the genuine power of optimism and how planting a seed of Greatness in one's mind can make them do tremendous things beyond their own imagination. Motivate the next person you see and lift up the world around you. When you lift up the world around you, the seed of Greatness you plant will shine like gold and create a ripple effect of transcendence and achievement. It was on that day that I began to see life clearly, and it opened my eyes to a world within a world of mass possibility and potential.

In this life, a million people are going to tell you that you can't do it, despite those who do lift you up. You will have to deal with naysayers and those who fail to see your aura of amazing talent and spirit. They'll think their ways of Success are the right ways when sometimes they are only projecting falsity and doubt in their own lives, trying to project it onto you. In your life, you'll be turned down, told no, rejected beyond belief, and the world will kick you until you give up and submit to letting your dreams pass you by. But you can never give up, and you can never allow life to beat you down and keep you there. Rocky Balboa famously said, "It ain't about how hard you can hit. It's about how hard you can get hit and keep moving forward. That's how winning is done!" Without that mentality for Success, the world will eat you up and spit you out.

    You have to be like Elon Musk. Elon Musk was severely bullied his entire life up until he founded PayPal and Tesla. He was told he could never be Successful by some of his greatest heroes in science, space exploration, entrepreneurialism, and quantum physics, but today is the man coined as the one who will send mankind to Mars. In an interview, when asked how he felt about the rejection from his heroes, tears filled his eyes as he stated how hurt he was to receive rejection and doubt from his heroes, yet Elon Musk became the 21st century's launch pad to make planetary colonization possible. He became a voice and an influential person in the 21st-century generation - a man who represented everything in proving the doubters wrong. When he sent the heaviest rocket known as Falcon 9, to the International Space Station in Operation Launch America, or when he sent 2,200 Starlink satellites to outer space while also working to send a ship of people to Mars for space travel, while simultaneously building the Hyperloop for underground transportation, Musk had Greatness on his mind. This is the formula for rising above the narrative that "it can't be done" or "it's impossible." Anything is possible in this life. You only need the right mindset, skills, foresight, connections, passion, and persistence.

I always found that proving the naysayers wrong was a mission I had to myself. It was never out of spite to prove people wrong. However, when I was told by some of my college professors that I would never become a great cop, and when I was told by friends that I couldn't make it to college after I was also told by teachers in middle school that I would never be successful in life because of my eccentric personality - it made me more infatuated for Success in all things that approached my table of challenges. I learned to love the haters and the naysayers because I always knew I would be able to prove them wrong and show the world my talents. There was never a better feeling than achieving those goals and one day unexpectedly hearing from those same naysayers, as they would suddenly congratulate me on my Success after years of telling me I'd never reach it. Today, I have reached it far over.

Perhaps even the naysayers plant a seed in our minds to do big things, as great people lead lives of quiet desperation as they ponder on the words of a naysayer and doubter. As once said in The Pursuit of Happyness, "Never let somebody tell you that you can't do something. If you want something, go get it. Period." Success is a journey of wins and losses similar to a long, hard-fought war. In the end, the war of life is won by the strong who refuse to give up. So in this life, when you are told you can't do it, it is in your power to prove them wrong and raise the bar for the next generation. Win the war. You know you can. Be the Victor. Never the victim. Prove them wrong and change the world.

Chapter 15: Creating a Legacy - How Do You Want To Be Remembered?

You get one life. One chance to make something of yourself and build a legacy that survives in the history books for generations to pass until the last days on Earth. All things will one day go away. But in this life, you can not squander the time you have. The average life is generally between 70 to 80 years old, and with future medical technology, human life will be able to last for centuries. But one day, you will die, and with that being said, you must create a legacy of your own accord. You must openly take on new opportunities and find the beauty in this chaotic life, despite the things that will knock you down and try to destroy your dreams.

Life is not about suffering every day, 9 to 5, and obeying the boss just because you have to get by. You get one life, and that's it. Beyond death, we know not what lies ahead. Only the dead know for certain what comes after the spirit leaves the body. While we are here on Earth, there are thousands of great ideas we conjure up in our minds without even keeping track of them. When you die, will you have regrets? Will you wish that you would have done what you wanted to in the past? When you breathe your last breath, are you currently able to say that you've accomplished your wildest dreams and completed your own personal mission on Earth? Have you fulfilled and finished the quest for Greatness without sorrow, resentment, or regret? If the answer is no, then you need to get started today and break free. Do everything you can before you are in the grave. You are never too old or young to do what you want, so go do it and be selfish about it. You get one life. When the clock runs out and when you've pumped your last heartbeat, what will be left behind? All things can be done if you have the will and the persistence to build and create your legacy. So the question stands, how do you want to be remembered?

When I was young, I wanted to be a professional baseball player, a Navy Seal, an actor, all of the above, like so many of us desire. But I knew my legacy was to save lives and protect the innocent. I knew my legacy was to educate and influence the masses. To defend those without a voice and to speak for the dead. To protect and serve my community and write about my own experiences. My legacy will die as a man of determination and great foresight. If I were to die today, just knowing that I was able to publish this book for you would be a major success in my life, and I will never die in vain knowing that I accomplished it. I will never die in vain because I learned early on that God is our Creator and perfect in his ways of design and making the impossible a reality. I spent my college years spending time working, planning, goal setting, writing, learning, and making memories with my Grandmother while she was still alive. I made sure to honor my Mother and even my Father, who I knew very little, if not at all. I forgave my enemies and learned to see the Greatness and potential of every human spirit. It is so important to create a legacy in your life, even if it is small in the eyes of the world around you. Build something for yourself because when you do, nothing can be stripped away from you. Build a future of promise and foundational Success by doing things like getting a diploma, a degree, building a business, marrying the love of your life, having children, adopting children, buying a home, learning about the Bible and other religions, and learning about the existential language of the cosmos. Achieve all the things people say cannot be done because they can be done. It is your will that will decide the transition from having dreams to making your dreams a living reality.

There are 8 billion people on planet Earth. The ideas that we have will last forever, and it is our job to make them possible while we are here and in the present. While we are here in a world of taking action, growing, learning, meeting new people, and finding the purpose in who we are, we will have the choice to transcend or remain victims of our own minds. We cannot let doubt or fear overtake the milestones we will face, and in order to achieve obtaining a 4-year degree, for example, takes focus and intention. If you seek Greatness, you will find it, and that is why I felt this book was so essential to writing. Future generations will read it and use it to help formulate their own lives. It is in hopes that you read this so you will better understand the laws of the universe and how to Succeed in not only college or entrepreneurship but also the hardest parts of life that challenge our deepest fears and darkest struggles. Remain one who consistently works towards your goals, and you will

Succeed in this life, reader. Remember every day that no day is promised. Ask yourself when you wake up how you want to be remembered, and that will be the first step towards the beginning of the rest of your life. May God be with you, may Success flourish in your future endeavors, and I wish you monumental Happiness. May this book remain close to you, your loved ones, and remember that anything is possible if you simply believe it with all your heart and soul. As once said by former President Donald J. Trump, "No dream is too big. No challenge is too great. Nothing we want for our future is beyond our reach". God Bless, reader, and may your life be filled with historical Success.

References

A. (2016). Suicide Statistics. Retrieved January 17, 2018, from

https://afsp.org/about-suicide/suicide-statistics/

Ayres, Crystal. "42 Shocking Police Brutality Statistics." Vittana.org, 2019,

https://vittana.org/42-shocking-police-brutality-statistics

Daskal, L. (2013, June 07). Leadership: What We Don't Know We Don't Know - Lolly Daskal | Leadership. Retrieved February 16, 2019, from

https://www.lollydaskal.com/leadership/leadership-what-we-dont-know-we-dont-know/

Eschner, K. (2017, April 13). What We Know About the CIA's Midcentury Mind-Control Project. Retrieved August 2, 2019, from

https://www.smithsonianmag.com/smart-news/what-we-know-about-cias-midcentury-mind-control-project-180962836/

Heidenry, M. (2019, June 23). How Much Does Home Staging Cost-and How Much Will You Gain? Retrieved June 26, 2019, from

https://www.realtor.com/advice/sell/how-much-does-home-staging-cost/

History.com Editors. (2009, November 9). Alexander the Great. Retrieved April 13, 2020, from https://www.history.com/topics/ancient-history/alexander-the-great

Isaac, M. (2017, June 21). Uber Founder Travis Kalanick Resigns as C.E.O. Retrieved January 30, 2019, from https://www.nytimes.com/2017/06/21/technology/uber-ceo-travis-kalanick.html

Penman, D., Kagan, J. (2019, May 25). Fiduciary. Retrieved June 26, 2019, from

https://www.investopedia.com/terms/f/fiduciary.asp

Koenig, M. (2019). Most Valuable Coins. Retrieved June 17, 2019, from

http://cointrackers.com/blog/11/most-valuable-coins/

Martin, E. (2017, July 10). The median home price in the U.S. is $200,000 - here's what that will get you across the country. Retrieved April 16, 2019, from

https://www.cnbc.com/2017/06/29/what-the-median-home-price-of-200000-will-get-you-across-the-us.html

Middleton, Y. (2018, December 27). 70 Highly Motivational Dwayne "The Rock" Johnson Quotes. Retrieved June 18, 2020, from

https://addicted2success.com/quotes/57-highly-motivational-dwayne-the-rock-johnson-quotes/

Ph.D, Emamzateh, A., & Selig, M. (n.d.). Depression. Retrieved January 17, 2019, from

https://www.psychologytoday.com/us/basics/depression

Realtor Salaries in Michigan. (2019, June 15). Retrieved June 26, 2019, from

https://www.indeed.com/salaries/Realtor-Salaries,-Michigan

Robotics, H. (2019). Sophia. Retrieved July 4, 2019, from

https://www.hansonrobotics.com/sophia/

Russell, J., & Russell, J. (2017, August 28). Who is new Uber CEO Dara Khosrowshahi? Retrieved January 30, 2019, from

https://techcrunch.com/2017/08/28/who-is-new-uber-ceo-dara-khosrowshahi/

Staff, G. (2018, July 13). Nostradamus Prophecies: 8 Predictions that Came True. Retrieved July 4, 2019, from https://www.gaia.com/article/8-need-know-nostradamus-prophecies

Trump, D., & Schwartz, T. (2017). Trump: The Art of the deal. New York: Ballantine Books.

UpNest. (n.d.). Average Michigan Real Estate Agent Commission Rate. Retrieved April 16, 2019, from https://www.upnest.com/1/post/average-michigan-real-estate-agent-commission-rate/

U.S News. (2019, June 26). Real Estate Agent Ranks Among Best Jobs of 2019. Retrieved 2019, from https://money.usnews.com/careers/best-jobs/real-estate-agent

Lite, G. (2020, January 12). The Lost Forbidden Teachings of Jesus. Retrieved March 13, 2020, from https://369news.net/2018/08/28/the-lost-forbidden-teachings-of-jesus/

White, D. (2020). Retrieved May 13, 2020, from https://study.com/academy/lesson/social-bond-theory-defintion-and-lesson.html

www.ingramcontent.com/pod-product-compliance
Lightning Source LLC
Chambersburg PA
CBHW050358120526
44590CB00015B/1740